BE BRIEF ABOUT IT

BOOKS BY ROBERT D. YOUNG
Published by The Westminster Press

Be Brief About It

Religious Imagination:
God's Gift to Prophets and Preachers

Encounter with World Religions

BE BRIEF ABOUT IT

by
ROBERT D. YOUNG

THE WESTMINSTER PRESS
Philadelphia

BOOK DESIGN BY DOROTHY ALDEN SMITH

First edition

Published by The Westminster Press®
Philadelphia, Pennsylvania

PRINTED IN THE UNITED STATES OF AMERICA

9 8 7 6 5 4 3 2 1

Library of Congress Cataloging in Publication Data

Young, Robert Doran, 1928–
   Be brief about it.

   Includes bibliographical references.
   1. Preaching. 2. Presbyterian Church—Sermons.
2. Sermons, American. I. Title.
BV4211.2.Y67   251   80–16436
ISBN 0–664–24321–5

Dedicated to my wife, Louisa,
COUNSELOR, CRITIC, AND CONFIDANT

CONTENTS

Acknowledgments   *9*

Introduction   *11*

PART I / REASONS FOR PREACHING
    BRIEFER SERMONS   15

  1. The Times Require Brevity   15

  2. Theology Sanctions Brevity   27

  3. Contagious Communication Utilizes Brevity   40

PART II / TEN GUIDELINES
    FOR BRIEF PREACHING   49

  1. Think Small   49

  2. Adopt a Poetry Model   54

  3. Select a Simple Unity   61

  4. Stay Close to the Original Inspiration   64

  5. Make the Point Quickly   72

  6. Trim the Cast   76

  7. Time's Up—Sign Off!   81

  8. Take Soundings   85

9. Feel Comfortable with Silence   95

10. Let the Listener Do the Traveling   100

PART III / DOES BREVITY COMPROMISE?   103

PART IV / SAMPLES   115

I Am the Way   117

Do You Want to Be Healed?   124

The Absurd Goodness of God   129

Keep Up the Good Work   135

Notes   *143*

ACKNOWLEDGMENTS

I am indebted to the people of West Chester, Pennsylvania, who have gathered for lunch and sermon at the Westminster Presbyterian Church during the seven Wednesdays of Lent. Their response and encouragement convinced me that communication took place, while the regimen itself affected for good the style of my other pulpit work. Pondering that Lenten experience became the basis for this book.

Along the way, I have had the privilege of enjoying the friendship of several editors. One took time to identify brevity as a fitting topic, another encouraged me to keep at the writing task; and others skillfully helped shape the final manuscript. They are Ed Cooperrider, Roland Tapp, and the staff of The Westminster Press.

Other good friends played their part. Dr. Frederick J. Wolter and Dr. Victor L. Baer read the manuscript and offered valuable suggestions. Dr. Wolter is a retired chemist, formerly with the Du Pont Company, who enjoys working with the English language. Dr. Baer was for many years on the staff of the Madison Avenue Presbyterian Church in association with George Buttrick and, later, David H. C. Read.

The typing was done by Mary Ellen Alton, a member of my church who can work effectively with people or manuscripts, making both the better for the encounter.

Apart from these, the influences on my life and thought have come from sources either too numerous or too hidden to identify. In fact, I am left with the uneasy feeling that a great company needs to be thanked which no one can number. God bless them all.

INTRODUCTION

This book is a plea for shorter sermons. Just as the twenty-minute sermon replaced the hourglass lecture of Colonial America, a new day invites ministers to trim down further. This invitation is not all bad. The need for brevity may lead to better communication of the gospel.

Anyone driving along the freeways a few years ago and catching an editorial of Rod MacLeish or Harry Reasoner will agree that much can be said in a matter of minutes. The speakers have trained themselves to communicate within a given space of time. These men deal with large amounts of material, but before they present it a mental compactor goes to work. The topic is condensed into small, solid, and easier-to-handle packages. The process of compacting should happen every time sermonic material is gathered.

The idea of brevity broke into my mind in conjunction with preaching a series of Lenten meditations to a noontime congregation from the business community. Within fifty minutes, this transient congregation bought lunch, ate, socialized, and left after a devotional period. Despite the utmost efficiency in handling the arrangements, I could find no more than eight or ten minutes for a sermon. At first, the task looked impossible; it was something like putting a model boat into a bottle. However, once my inner pacer had regulated itself, I found that a significant message could be presented. Not only was the period of time sufficient, but the ten-minute limit contributed to the intensity of the message. The structure helped the urgency, which became the driving force for whatever I wanted to say. With this in mind, I continued to work on the Sunday morning sermons, not reducing them to eight minutes or ten, but chipping off minutes where possible, and sharpening their style. Once again, style and brevity were intertwined with content, and the result was a plus for communication.

Brevity, in itself, seems like a trite theme for the homiletician. A table of contents in any published volume of the Lyman Beecher lectures on preaching will list a wide gamut of other topics: expository preaching, topical preaching, outlining the message, illustrating the message, planning a year's pulpit work, and so forth. The subjects go on and on, and many have far more hard-core content than the seemingly light subject of sermon length. However, all subjects related to good preaching are so intertwined that to pick any one is to find others tied on the same line. This was my experience in examining the theme of brevity.

Furthermore, all parts of the sermonic enterprise, whether trite or weighty, must be reexamined today to see if they have fallen into disrepair. Recently we passed through a period when sermonizing was not valued highly by ministers. We thought the action was in the city chambers, or in street marches, or in community councils. The sermon took a backseat to social activism. Without turning our backs on the lasting results of such activism, we ministers must confess that it took its toll on us as preachers. We did not give the sermon the priority of our time, our reading, or our skill. Along with this eclipse of the sermon we also neglected the critical evaluation of many parts of the homiletical discipline that former generations took for granted. How long a sermon ought to be simply was not discussed. In our day it is appropriate to factor out brevity from other aspects of preaching and examine it, leaving those other aspects constant. This is what I have done.

The line of argument begins with the question, "Why this particular theme?" What reasons make it important? I have distinguished three, though there may be more. One reason presses in from society. The mood of the times requires a brief, terse style. A second reason, oddly enough, springs up from theology itself. There is what might be termed a theology of style, in which form—as well as content—is shaped by the Biblical revelation. Theology suggests that the gospel message might be handled better in brief, hinting speech than in the long-drawn-out prose of the lecture room. A third reason is quite practical. Brief speech, by the very act of saying much within strict limits, builds an intensity that makes for better communication. To communicate effectively is the fervent wish of everyone who enters the pulpit to say something about the God who has visited us in Jesus Christ.

On the basis of these three reasons, I shall proceed to give ten guidelines or suggestions that can help in the preparation of briefer sermons. This section forms the "how" of brevity, though it is sprinkled with theoretical observations about the nature of preaching. Then I will examine a critical question. Does brevity compromise either the message or the messenger? On the one hand, do brief sermons cater to the market in an attempt to win back a lost audience at any price? If so, they might be more obedient to the idol of popularity than to the name of Jesus. On the other hand, will brief sermons destroy the minister, making the scholarship he or she prized in seminary no longer necessary in the practical work of preaching? These questions must be faced with candor.

In the last section, I attempt to demonstrate the method by including a few sample sermons. The preaching time for each of them is eight to ten minutes. However, not all brief sermons need be that short. Brevity is a relative term—and in two ways. A sermon may be brief by the clock, as compared with the same sermon extended twice as long. Or it may be brief psychologically, as when the listener is not aware of the clock at all. It is hoped that the sermons included are brief in both these ways.

1

THE TIMES REQUIRE BREVITY

The basic sociological reason for brevity in the pulpit is that the American audience is short of time. This, in itself, prods the preacher to be brief. The situation in America might be different if there was a tradition of daily siestas, afternoon teas, or even Zen meditation. However, this is not so. When morning comes, the arteries of the city throb. Ceaseless activity is omnipresent, and the pace continues until night. From morning to night salespeople jump into cars; secretaries pump typewriter keys; telephone operators push calls through; pilots take off and land. Papers cross desks, jam files, are processed for delivery. Computers blink their lights and spew out messages at 220 pages per minute. Preachers live and preach in this kind of world. They are somewhere caught in the whirring, and must figure out what to say and how to say it in a world where whirl is king.

There is, of course, a temptation to protest this frenzy. Why not blow the whistle and call a halt to the mad pace of things? The appeal for this type of protest is strong, and getting stronger. Some of it blows in from the Orient. The image of the quiet monk, alert in contemplation, haunts the cigar-chewing, brisk-paced executive as he signs up for a course in transcendental meditation. Another wind of protest comes from the *What Makes Sammy Run?* type of novel, which describes the mad pace and wonders what is behind it—and asks if the pace is worth it. The author of *The Peter Principle* questioned the automatic upward mobility of people in business, realizing that many get promoted to levels where they do not function as effectively as if they had remained in some former job. True enough. However, many who found the "principle" appealing were or could be quite effective in higher positions, but they do not choose to move because the pace is fast enough where they are. Dr. Peter himself claims that teaching is his forte, and he intends to stay in teaching, even though he could function well as an administrator. Once in a while (so he claims) the dean drops in to his classroom to urge him to become head of the department. Whereupon, the sociologist-author bends against the wall, drools, lets his cigarette slither to the side of his mouth while he mumbles drunken inanities. This, until the dean backs out into the hall, wondering why he was crazy enough to enter in the first place. That's a creative protest against further pressure. A willingness to say no to the perpetual motion machine.

Even the humorist steps forward to protest frenzy. Poet Virginia Brasier, writing in the style of Ogden Nash, twitted this American weakness, which she saw in the last generation:

> This is the age
> Of the half read page
> And the quick hash
> And the mad dash
> The bright night
> With the nerves tight
> The plane hop
> With the brief stop
> The lamp tan
> In a short span
> The big shot
> In a good spot
> And the brain strain
> And the heart pain
> And the cat naps
> Till the spring snaps
> And the fun's done.[1]

With protest taking so many forms, perhaps we preachers should join in and encourage all those who want to get back to a simpler style of life. We could attempt to contribute to the "greening of America," and point to the values of art and nature and slow-paced camaraderie. Perhaps the energy shortages will put the brake on our unnecessary darting to and fro, cancel a few committee meetings, make us appreciate our neighborhoods without the need for the weekend exodus. Or perhaps afternoon siestas are not too far-fetched, if, as is now being predicted, sometime in the 1980's, Spanish-speaking immigrants will constitute 10 percent of the American population. Could the new immigrants introduce some mañana philosophy as the leaven to our social dough? Don't count on it, or rush out to buy sombreros. The protest against frenzy might be there, and gain some adherents. Yet the nation can't go home again to village life, except for brief vacations. All such protest—whether deriving from the Bible or the Orient, whether expressed by poet or novelist, whether somber or touched with biting humor—is probably a voice crying in the wilderness. The realistic fact is that the American audience is short of time. It always has been, and in recent times America has only raised its tempo from fast to frantic. Wishing won't change that elemental fact.

Such resignation to the "short of time" syndrome was reinforced recently by Joseph Sittler in a remarkable essay, "Space and Time in the American Religious Experience."[2] The basic idea was developed first by Sidney Mead, and expanded by Sittler. Both men feel that Europe and America differ in the way they view space and time. Europe is short on space, but long on time. Europe is compact. The boundaries of different countries are close together. The limitation to expansion has been set for centuries. There is no room to stretch out in vast new territory. On the other hand, Europeans' apprehension of time is not confined, since their history goes back many centuries. Dark Ages, Middle Ages, Modern Age, Future Age—all fit along the endless time line and encourage patience, compromise, adaptability, respect for ancestry, and other time-conscious virtues. The American perspective is quite different. In America, space stretches out endlessly, but time is in short supply. Until recently, for instance, there was always some new spatial frontier.

There was the Western frontier, the Prairie, Alaska, the Islands. Then, when terrestrial expansion had run its course, exploration of outer space began. Therefore, in America the need to conserve space has not been as strong as in Europe.

However, time is another matter for us. Time is of the essence in America. We are constantly running out of it. We see it as "our" time, unrelated to generations past or yet to come. What we do must be done now. Nothing escapes that penchant for immediacy. If the problem is worldwide unbelief, then we will win the world in our generation, or in a particular time span. If the problem is energy, we will look for a solution that will be handled temporarily by a regulation from Washington until our scientists can settle it once and for all next year. This is the basic quickstep by which we dance through life, and this mentality did not start in the raucous '60s or in the expansive period following World War II. Shortness of time and hurry to achieve have been with us since our nation was founded.

To back up this observation, Mead found an entry in the journal of Francis Parkman, famous explorer of the nineteenth century, and one whose descriptions of buffalo and Indians and prairies are still classic. The observation was written somewhere along the Oregon Trail, on a day when Parkman had shot an antelope. The explorer wrote: "When I stood by his side, the antelope turned his expiring eye upward. It was like a beautiful woman's, dark and bright. Fortunately, I am in a hurry! thought I; I might be troubled by remorse if I had time for it."[3] Parkman wrote his journal in the 1840's, when the pace of life was supposedly slower. Apparently that was not so.

Or, this account given in a poem by Stephen Vincent Benét points in the same direction. The poem is called *Western Star,* and describes a caravan moving west. A little girl dies. It is winter, and with difficulty the group gives her a suitable burial. But there is no time to stay and mourn.

> There is no time to grieve now, there is no time—
> There is only time for labor in the cold.[4]

Even then, in the pioneering days of the last century, shortness of time was in the American blood. It did not come with the invention of the Model T or the airplane. It was no doubt nourished by the open spaces, which gave the illusion that totally new beginnings could be made, with hard work and quick movement. The advice "Go west, young man" was given, not that the young man might help the generations to follow by an increment of industry, but rather that he might subdue the forest, build an empire, make a name, and come back with a million, all in one lifetime. Such an attitude, nourished in our history and our heroes, is not soon eradicated. We are a nation on the run. Better to recognize this in preaching than to tilt at the windmill of the American experience. We preach in an environment where time is of the essence.

Therefore, a minister entering the pulpit should write at the top of the manuscript, "I ain't got long to stay here." To be conscious of time, to realize that something weighty must be said in a set period of time, is a first step to relevant preaching. The very idea of brevity conjures up crisp words, tight language, orderly argument, deft illustration. The congregation reinforces this idea and prods us to brevity. They won't tolerate sermons that get up at the crack of noon. "Up—on with it—sit down" is the silent order they give us.

Oddly enough, though time is limited, Americans do give it away in large amounts for things they like. Indoor tennis courts are scheduled from early, pre-work hours until late at night. A several-hour drive to the ski resort is easily managed on weekends. At golf courses there are lines waiting to get on the first tee. The boat mooring areas are alive from spring through fall. Cranes lift boats in and out of the water. Trailers push boats down the ramp and receive them again. The summer house needs and receives as much attention as the winter house, and for more and more weeks every year. For all these things, Americans give freely of their most precious commodity—time. Why doesn't the sermon evoke the same kind of giving?

Even passive ventures eat up hours, and Americans seem glad to have it so. The sports calendar is filled and so are the stands.

Each sport extends its season and overlaps the other sports which wait in the wings. The World Series is played after the football season opens. Basketball and hockey playoffs run well into baseball's spring training period. No American who is a sports enthusiast begrudges the time it takes to watch and cheer. The same devotion is given to television. It is estimated that Americans who live to old age will have spent the equivalent of six years in front of the television set, an awesome amount of time to be a spectator. Why, then, the difficulty in giving a mere hour to worship and a sermon? An octogenarian who was in church every Sunday of his life would not have devoted more than a half year of equivalent time. Again, why doesn't the sermon evoke the gift of time from audiences that are so profligate in giving it to sports and television?

The question is complex, and the church may be more sinned against than sinning. However, one valuable insight is coming to the surface. A great number of unchurched Americans see the church as too ingrown and self-serving, not worth scheduling into other active or passive enterprises they so much enjoy. This came out in a recent Gallup poll of unchurched Americans.[5] Gallup found this group not as irreligious as many supposed. A large number even professed having had a sudden conversion. They knew the language of religious experience and felt positive toward it. But they did not feel positive toward the church. The church was antiquated, not relevant to its time, more interested in maintaining organizational machinery than in nurturing religious experience. Therefore they did not schedule churchgoing into their busy routines. For them, belonging was not necessary for believing. In fact, the church was judged so far out of touch with vital religion that the unchurched might have enjoyed the quip of Jonathan Swift, "If Christianity were to be abolished, in time even the church would suffer."

This criticism of the church by the unchurched helps to explain why the masses rush by the church rather than rush into it. The church is often the gray stone turtle that sits in the sun on valuable downtown property. What is it doing? In many cases, not much other than sunning itself, and occasionally moving, much too slowly. The disenchanted see the church as having too much machinery, being serviced by too many mechanics, costing too much to run, and producing too little that is marketable. As an old proverb puts it, there is "too much shifting of the plates for the fewness of the victuals."

The disenchanted also note that the church has done little to prevent war, to cope with drugs, to shape government ethics. Furthermore—at a time when we are faced with gigantic problems of energy waste, food scarcity, urban clutter, welfare breakdown, racial inequities—the millions of sermonic words usually stay in the relatively safe area of personal piety. Even there the sermon is not noticeably effective. Children opt for drugs, parents opt for divorce, and boredom remains the number one killer. What have those billions of sermon words accomplished? Therefore, it is not a time for those who love the church to hurl salvos at those who don't. Perhaps repentance is called for, since there is good reason for the anti-institutional mood that Gallup records.

Recently, while traveling in England, my wife and I worshiped in Durham Cathedral, where history permeates the walls and the massive Norman columns. This is what we saw. The clergy, about twenty in number, processed into the choir seats, facing each other, and proceeded to recite the Scriptures, offer prayers of the day, chant hymns, and make antiphonal responses. When the liturgy was finished, they recessed, led by the beadle. Worship had taken place in a pure form just as it had for many centuries. In fact, such services have been held at Durham without interruption since the eleventh century, and the clergy take pride in that achievement. After the service, one clergyman explained that their role as clergy was to preserve the Christian faith from erosion from generation to generation. Durham was to be the model for surrounding churches. That was the work to which they were committed, to keep the tradition in as pure a form as possible.

Now, it is easy to be critical of another worship style, and perhaps relevance is too much to expect when the remains of the Venerable Bede lie buried in the cloister of Durham, a constant reminder of tradition. However, one can't blame the English if they function outside the cathedral, and see little need to go into it. My mind went back to Old Mortality, that character in Scott's novel who spent his days relettering inscriptions on tombstones that had been defaced by the weather. He wanted to make the words stand out for the next generation, certainly a worthy work, but only for those of a certain mind-set. I also thought of the American churches that have the monastic mentality and hope to ride out the current antichurch mood while waiting for better times for old-time faith. Such a monastic philosophy, of doing it the way we have always done it, would probably leave the American church marked by the antiquarian symbols that dominate English cathedrals: the museum, the curio shop, and the collection box for roof repair. No wonder T. S. Eliot put the layman's complaint in those sarcastic words, "Too many churches, and too few chop-houses."[6]

Any institutional self-serving deserves to be ignored. It is not worth the time and effort of the masses to perpetuate it. However, there are still other insidious ways the clergy reflect to the congregation that they do not understand that there is a different mood and tempo "out there." The style of the minister's speech in the sermon will do this regardless of the content. Every time the minister uses verbal profusion or antique phrases in making an introduction or in dedicating a baby or in polishing the third point of the sermon, modern congregants have further reason to tune out. Every quote from a Romantic poet, every illustration from classical Greece, every flourish of old-style oratory, confirms the message—the gray stone Gothic building is staffed by a gray stone Gothic clergyman. The minister's verbal manner is slightly out of step with the times, when to be out of step is to be out of mind.

This picture of the slightly overweight, slightly verbose, slightly affected clergyman is the ideal setup for so many *New Yorker* cartoons. They love to put a pinprick in such pomposity. For instance, one cartoon I keep in my desk drawer shows a preacher giving an exhortation on television. He is fat, pompous, and in clericals. His Bible is in one hand; he pounds the air with the other. His gestures are so violent they nearly jar loose his pince-nez. The listener in this cartoon is a beef 'n' beer character slouched in an easy chair, with a leg thrown over the arm. He is drinking a can of beer and eating a sandwich. His comment to the television preacher? "You tell 'em pal!" That, and an incredulous grin. This pictures in sharpest satire the apathetic mood that exists in many who sit in the pews. The minister is no longer the person in the community who commands the highest intellectual respect. He is no longer at the center of the town's power structure. He is not usually the Amos type, hated for his fierce proclamation of the truth. He is ignored while the busy world rushes through its program; or, if not ignored, then made the object of *New Yorker* humor.

What is to be done to correct this, or at least to realize that we have a problem?

First of all, accept what is legitimate of the criticism that comes, whether from the Gallup poll or *The New Yorker,* our neighbors or our teen-age children. Perhaps a pin might prick any bubble of pomposity. Stand in the shoes of the unchurched Americans. Try to grasp how the sermon is coming through, not just in content but in style. Play the devil's advocate with your own pulpit offerings. Ask if they are really worth the time to hear, as over against getting an early start for the shore.

Anthony Trollope, who is enjoying a revival of readership, played the critic of clergy in the mid-nineteenth century. This choice attack is an aside in the story of *Barchester Towers* that is both dated and yet highly relevant:

> There is, perhaps, no greater hardship at present inflicted on mankind in civilized and free countries, than the necessity of listening to sermons. No one but a preaching clergyman has, in these realms, the power of compelling an audience to sit silent, and be tormented. No one but a preaching clergyman can revel in platitudes, truisms, and untruisms, and yet receive, as his undisputed privilege, the same respectful demeanour as though words of impassioned eloquence, or persuasive logic, fell from his lips. Let a professor of law or physic find his place in a lecture-room and there pour forth jejune words and useless empty phrases and he will pour them forth to empty benches. Let a barrister

attempt to talk without talking well, and he will talk but seldom. A judge's charge need be listened to perforce by none but the jury, prisoner, and gaoler. A member of Parliament can be coughed down or counted out. Town-councillors can be tabooed. But no one can rid himself of the preaching clergyman. . . . We desire, nay, we are resolute, to enjoy the comfort of public worship; but we desire also that we may do so without an amount of tedium which ordinary human nature cannot endure with patience; that we may be able to leave the house of God, without that anxious longing for escape, which is the common consequence of common sermons. . . .

And here I must make a protest against the pretence, so often put forward by the working clergy, that they are overburdened by the multitude of sermons to be preached. We are all too fond of our own voices, and a preacher is encouraged in the vanity of making his heard by the privilege of a compelled audience. His sermon is the pleasant morsel of his life, his delicious moment of self-exaltation. "I have preached nine sermons this week," said a young friend to me the other day, with hand languidly raised to his brow, the picture of an overburdened martyr. "Nine this week, seven last week, four the week before. I have preached twenty-three sermons this month. It is really too much." "Too much, indeed," said I, shuddering; "too much for the strength of any one." "Yes," he answered meekly, "indeed it is; I am beginning to feel it painfully." "Would," said I, "you could feel it—would that you could be made to feel it." But he never guessed that my heart was wrung for the poor listeners.[7]

The piece is dated in that Trollope assumes people are still going to endure church, no matter what. Yet it is a distant mirror in which we clergy can see ourselves and make the necessary adjustments.

Secondly, attend to the message, that it might be in touch with both the gospel and the times. There is a dearth of the Word of God. Even the unchurched recognized this. Their criticism was not that the gospel was unneeded, but only that it was not necessarily found in church.

Just that, the recognition that the gospel is needed, should encourage those of us who by profession are charged to proclaim it. This means to proclaim the full gospel, with time spent at the cross and empty tomb, in the exodus and among the prophets. It must include doctrine, story, ethics, and eschatology. It must hold out hope for me and my relationships and the world in which I function. We have a mandate to pronounce a full meaning to the word "salvation."

Not long ago, the counsel was otherwise. In a well-written book of the 1960's, J. C. Hoekendijk felt that the church had been too verbal. He advised the church to be a presence, a listening church, with a heavy stress on serving the world, no questions asked. The church must, according to Hoekendijk, get outside the walls, and be content to be *there*. It should not try to say anything important. He states:

> The proclamation to the outside can never be a rehash of the sermon. Structurally it is something entirely different from a sermon.
>
> To state this more strongly: it is an illusion to suppose that communication of the gospel will be possible only through the word. . . . What is asked of us is that we resist every temptation to engage in an exclusively or even primarily verbal communication.[8]

Hoekendijk's advice was understandable in the turbulent decade of the '60s, when Americans were never certain where the next race riot or campus violence would erupt. Fortunately, that era has passed. So have the excesses of the nonmetaphysical philosophies and theologies that tuned in to those times. The "death of God" language that coincided with the dearth of preaching has now moved offshore and out to sea. As a result, the weather is much clearer for preaching, to ponder what is the gospel message, and then proclaim it.

Granted we have a message, the third question to be faced is: How shall we shape it for today's audience? What style should it have for people on the move? These are not Trollope's compatriots, who will stay by the church on good days and bad. Most of them have already weighed the church and its typical message and found them wanting. These people are used to minute-long editorials with everything extraneous chipped away. They like digests of news, digests of books, and brief memos. They like short discourses, popular lectures, practical help. They want the meaning of life to be spoken in this context and (what is not always realized) in this style. This latter subject, the need for a style that matches the mood of the times, is the burden of this book.

We don't usually look to theology to say anything about sermon style. When we speak of theology—whether Arminian or Calvinistic, Biblical or philosophical, Barthian or Tillichian, dispensational or covenantal, "death of God" or process theology—we usually think of the ideas the theology presents. The content is first and foremost in our minds. We never question the style in relation to content. Theologians can write in a poetic style as Novalis did, or in intricate prose as the Niebuhrs; they can write numerous monographs like Cullmann, or a multiple-volume work like Barth. Style is left to each person's individual taste and is hardly noticed as having anything to do with the theology presented. Yet this may be quite wrong and overlook an important fact. The method of communication may be intimately bound up with the content to be communicated. Two questions, then, can be raised about sermons. First, what content should they possess? In other words, what is the gospel message? Second, what style best conveys the gospel message?

If our analysis of the American mood is correct, then preachers need to get in and out of their subjects more quickly. Brevity is called for. But does Christian theology concur? Is the gospel treated fairly when conveyed in this manner, or is it handicapped? It is one thing to be brief because the times demand it, because you might get more of a hearing. It is quite another to be brief because Christian theology sanctions it. Without a theological dimension, brevity may be a sellout to popularity, a catering to the market. However, if theology indicates that brevity is a fit style for the gospel's proclamation and the times also demand it, then preachers are foolish to ignore this twofold persuasion. Therefore, let us now look into an often neglected topic—a theology of style.

2

THEOLOGY SANCTIONS BREVITY

Granted that Americans are in a hurry to get to their various recreations. Granted that the mood of the times is apathetic toward both church and sermon. These facts in themselves are not strong enough to support the case for brevity. If, on the other hand, a rationale for brevity grows out of the Biblical revelation, a more solid foundation is laid. Brevity would not then be a matter of expediency so much as faithfulness to God. Theological sense would reinforce common sense and become a far more compelling voice in the preacher's ear than any raucous sounds from the cultural wilderness. What, then, does our revelation say on the subject?

First of all, note that Jesus mastered the art of brevity. The "long" discourses in the Gospel of John are not long at all, even assuming they were spoken at one time. Fifteen minutes will handle the upper room discourses in John; another fifteen, the Sermon on the Mount in Matthew. At other times, a parable is tossed into an occasion. A proverbial saying is offered to memory or conscience. Jewish tradition is reshaped, filled with new wine, and set on the table for drinking. Nothing is ponderous, nothing frothy. Points are made quickly, and wrapped in manageable parcels for easy carrying.

Why did Jesus take this approach? Were his hearers intellectually below par? Or was Jesus paying the price of being an itinerant—too much on the move to frame a definitive message, then write it down? No such thing. Jesus knew what he was about in method and style as well as in saying what was on his mind. His message came from the bubbling fountain of origins, not from books or the dusty lecture hall. His words were lively and life-giving. He compressed eternity into vivid phrases and offered them to the imagination of his hearers. He did not overtalk, because a profusion of words would have lulled his audience to sleep, making them neither ardent followers nor aggressive opponents.

In an apt expression, poet Marianne Moore says that "Expanded explanation tends to spoil the lion's leap."[9] A full explanation of Jesus' parables, a longer form of the Sermon on the Mount with illustrations and applications, a reasoned defense of the otherwise "hard sayings," would blunt the edge of Jesus' message. Christ, Lion of the tribe of Judah, would soon become Christ the Tabby, or Christ the Teddy Bear. Thus, Jesus speaks briefly and with great precision. To quote Moore again: "The lion's leap would be mitigated almost to harmlessness if the lion were clawless. Just so, precision is both impact and exactitude, as with surgery."[10] Take this insight back to the Gospels and examine Jesus' teaching. His words are not just brief, but exact. It would be brief to say, "It is not nice to be hypocritical"; it is exact to say, "Judge not, that you be not judged." A short platitude such as "Be forgiving" is not the same as the prayer, "Forgive us our debts, as we forgive our debtors." A short lecture to hypocrites doesn't have the punch of the one-liner, "Let him who is without sin among you be the first to throw a stone." As with all the sayings and stories of Jesus, those memorable teachings land on our conscience so that we can't get away. There is nothing to spoil the lion's leap.

What is true for the teaching of Jesus is true of other parts of Scripture. Despite the variety of the types of literature, compression is at work in many places. The proverbs, of course, have a terse quality; the Minor Prophets are minor only because they lack quantity. The psalms are short because they pack imaginative language, as one would expect. And the letters of Paul are brief because that is the quality of letters. In these writings one would expect compression, but it is also at work in areas where one would not expect it. A period of time that extends from the creation to Abraham, literally eons, is covered in eleven chapters of Genesis. The socioeconomic conditions that led to a downturn in the fortunes of the Hebrews in Egypt is neatly summed up in the phrase, "There arose a new king over Egypt, who did not know Joseph." Even the more straightforward telling of history is marked by parsimony of speech. There is not the expansiveness of a Cecil B. DeMille in telling the story of David's affair with Bathsheba and Nathan's judgment which followed. It is brief and direct: "In the spring of the year, the time when kings go forth to battle, David sent Joab, and his servants with him, and all Israel; and they ravaged the Ammonites, and besieged Rabbah. But David remained at Jerusalem. It happened, late one afternoon, when David arose from his couch . . ." (II Sam. 11:1–2). A concise introduction to a drama, with the built-in coloration of judgment. The masses are doing their duty, struggling in battles; the leader is lounging back home.

We think of the Bible as a long book. It really is not long at all. It contains the acts of God, and reflections on those acts in a variety of literary styles, but always under compression. In one chapter, with a minimum of adjectives and a maximum of action verbs, John describes the crucifixion. He begins, "Then Pilate took Jesus and scourged him," moves through the trial, out along the Via Dolorosa, up to the place of a skull, through six hours of crucifixion, and finally to the tomb, ending with the words, "They laid Jesus there." All that in forty-two verses! Not a wasted word or action. Nothing exhaustive, and yet you feel "the lion's leap."

The same can be said for the Bible's finale. A description of the City of God. Think of the temptation to describe this with a profusion of words. The assignment would be to describe this city, its origins, its features, its meaning for us who sweat out our day in history, its relation to the Creator, its benefits for those caught in modern cities—and besides all this, to make the city more beautiful than a resort and better supplied than a farm. Even if the aim of the assignment were to give only a brief description, it is hard to believe the Biblical writer does this in the equivalent of six English sentences! Apparently the revelation does not need to be exhaustive to be effective.

Let's state that another way. I do not want to imply that the Bible is effective despite its compressed message. This would mean the Bible was handicapped by its method. Quite the reverse. The lengthening process would not say more, but less. This is because of the enormous amount of meaning that significant words pick up in a living tradition. Such words are best left undefined so that the vitality of their historic significance can make a thousand computer connections in the minds of the hearers.

For instance, consider the word "covenant," which Jesus used at the Last Supper. "This cup . . . is the new covenant in my blood." The covenant theme goes back to Israel's dim beginnings, so that the more you know of those beginnings, the more lively your imagination becomes. "Covenant" recalls stories of the patriarchs, with specific scenes of Abraham's altar, Isaac's near-sacrifice, Jacob's dream ladder, Joseph's imprisonment in Egypt. "Covenant" speaks of the initiative of God that came when Abraham set out in faith, and when Israel was in Egypt's land, and when the people hung up their harps by the waters of Babylon and sat down to cry. "Covenant" recalls Sinai, the law to be followed, the law that blessed, and the law that was broken. It suggests acts of allegiance by families and nations. It operated when Joshua promised, "As for me and my house, we will serve the LORD." It also was behind those words of national significance, "If my people who are called by my name humble themselves, and pray and seek my face, and turn from their wicked ways, then I will hear from heaven, and will forgive their sin and heal their land" (II Chron. 7:14). The covenant prompts allegiance by those under it. Then, too, other suggestions grow as Israel's history unfolds. Jeremiah and Ezekiel promise a new covenant. This time the covenant will not be an external one. It will be written not on stone, but in the viscera, written on the heart.

If these are some of the meanings of covenant, for Jesus to use the word in a brief sentence, "This is the new covenant in my blood," is to draw on a wealth of meaning too vast to be incorporated in words. By deliberately not being more specific, more is conveyed than by elaborating. An absence of extensive language allows the whole army of meanings to march over the mind and possess the territory. To specify is to restrict. Explicitness is the enemy both of brevity and of fuller meaning.

Let's look at one more example of Biblical brevity, the familiar phrase "kingdom of God." Jesus never defined it, even though he gave it added content. By leaving it free of exact definition, he added to its force while saving miles of verbiage in the process. Already by New Testament times the word had an earthly quality given by remembering David and the kings. It also had a Camelot quality, calling to mind all the prophecies of the coming Messiah. It spoke of a golden age past and present when justice would start to flow like waters. While leaving the full weight of connotations intact, by analogy Jesus pushed out the meaning still farther. The kingdom of heaven is "like." But, what is it like? Theologian-novelist Dorothy Sayers tries to form the composite. It is full of dartings, and paradox, and flashes of light.

"You cannot point to existing specimens, saying 'Lo, here!' or 'Lo, there!' You can only experience it. But, what is it like, so that when we experience it, we may recognize it? Well, it is a change, like being born again and re-learning everything from the start. It is secret, living power—like yeast. It is something that grows, like seed. It is precious like buried treasure, like a rich pearl, and you have to pay for it. It is a sharp cleavage through the rich jumble of things which life presents: like fish and rubbish in a draw net, like wheat and tares; like wisdom and folly; and it carries with it a kind of menacing finality; it is new, yet in a sense it was always there—like turning out a cupboard and finding there your own childhood as well as your present self; it makes demands, it is like an invitation to a royal banquet —gratifying, but not to be disregarded, and you have to live up to it; where it is equal, it seems unjust, where it is just it is clearly not equal—as with the single pound, the diverse talents, the labourers in the vineyard, you have what you bargained for; it knows no compromise between an uncalculating mercy and a terrible justice—like the unmerciful servant, you get what you give; it is helpless in your hands like the King's Son, but if you slay it, it will judge you; it was from the foundations of the world; it is to come; it is here and now; it is within you. It is recorded that the multitude sometimes failed to understand."[11]

There is nothing systematic in Jesus' presentation of the kingdom of God. You can't go away saying, "I've got it," meaning you have gathered a few well-ordered statements. Yet, you have got it in a more lasting and varied way than ever. It has the force of analogy, of Old Testament history, of the basic image of God ruling. The open-endedness of the phrase can be used significantly in multiple ways. It can guide the Christian revolutionist who looks for the righteousness of agrarian reform in South America; it can prod the members of a family to seek better communication so that the kingdom can be among them; it can remind the executive to face her priorities so that she might seek first the kingdom; it can encourage the problem drinker to believe that the authority of God is also the power to overcome; it can help the politician to look beyond current legislation knowing there is a kingdom to come on earth as it is in heaven; it can lift the spirit of the dying to see "spires away on the world's rim." Any definition of the kingdom of God that specifically took the meaning down one of these channels in the interests of preciseness would rule out other meanings that still cry out for understanding.

It is amazing how movements that begin with a lilt often end in fatigue, mainly through overtalk. R. R. Marett, the well-known anthropologist, put this observation in a memorable sentence. He noted that religion at the start is "danced out before it is thought out." Jesus, who wrote nothing, moved in speech as if in a dance, displaying artful turns, grace, controlled enthusiasm, excellent timing. The Gospels that caught his words preserved this simplicity. Paul goes the next step. Paul amplifies, theologizes, but still with open-ended language, hinting speech, incomplete argument, swift flow of imagery. But it is not long before the freshness of the gospel is lost. Ponderous fathers and Angelic Doctors enter from the wings with lead feet and no imagination. They write religious tomes. Thus, the *Summa* of Thomas Aquinas follows the fresh religious "absurdity" of Tertullian; and the scholastic seventeenth century follows the vital sixteenth. As night follows day, long exposition follows firsthand experience, and always the liveliness of the gospel is choked.

The problem in overtalking the gospel, from a theological point of view, has nothing to do with the short attention span of modern Americans—what we have called the mood of the times. More to the point, long theological statement betrays its subject. It deadens, while professing that its subject is the God of life. Furthermore, it continues to commit hypocrisy by pretending to know more than it does. The words of the argument, spun out endlessly, are more like the cloth in The Emperor's New Clothes. In the long run, the cloth does not cover the subject at all, even though everyone says it does.

Let us take a simple example. How much quantity of language is needed to do justice to the nature of God? We are given in the Bible a revelation that tells of God's mighty acts to save the world. If you want to convey this from the pulpit, how long a sermon will be needed? Fifteen minutes? A half hour? An all-day lecture? Does not all speech stand humble, eyes down, before such a mystery? If it does not, then "He who sits in the heavens laughs" as surely as the beef 'n' beer character in the *New Yorker* cartoon snickers and says, "You tell 'em pal!" On the surface, it would seem that the more time is used to explain the revelation, the better. Theologically speaking, the reverse might be true.

Consider the well-known description of God given in the Westminster Confession, and ask whether this really gets it all together. In part, it reads:

> There is but one only living and true God, who is infinite in being and perfection, a most pure spirit, invisible, without body, parts, or passions, immutable, immense, eternal, incomprehensible, almighty, most wise, most holy, most free, most absolute, working

> all things according to the counsel of his own immutable and most
> righteous will, for his own glory; most loving, gracious, merciful,
> long-suffering, abundant in goodness and truth, forgiving iniq-
> uity, transgression, and sin; the rewarder of them that diligently
> seek him, and withal most just and terrible in his judgments,
> hating all sin, and who will by no means clear the guilty. (II, 1)

We have now covered (or partly covered, since the paragraph
goes on) the nature of God. Oh? Is it not true once again that
the more the paragraph is extended, the less it is really the living
God who is under consideration? The Bible never reads like the
Westminster Confession. It merely drops hints in words like
"shepherd," "rock," "fortress," "everlasting arms." For the
rest, "What shall I answer thee? I lay my hand on my mouth"
(Job 40:4). The eternal God refuses to be caught in a net of
words, even though it is through words that the tradition comes
alive and is passed on.

We deal with a subject that is paradoxical. The gospel defies
language even while it insists upon being spoken. The mystics
are in touch with this. That is why they spend time in silent
meditation, and why Zen monks use those weighty puzzles
called koans, and Hasidic teachers use riddles. That is why
Buddha often stood in silence and refused to be lured into
speculation. How much language can adequately circumscribe
the Almighty? Shall a chapter do it, or a book of systematics?
God hides behind such verbiage and then escapes. Some recall
of Job is in order: "Who is this that darkens counsel by words
without knowledge? . . . Where were you when I laid the foundation of the earth?" (Job 38:2, 4). Or perhaps T. S. Eliot has it
right: "Words strain, crack and sometimes break, under the
burden . . ."[12] This being so, thoughtful brevity is a better vehicle
for the topic of God than any great amount of verbal extension.
As the Oriental proverb puts it, "He who says does not know;
he who knows does not say" (does not say too much, that is).
Incompleteness—hinting speech—with room for pondering,
may be more of a boon than a handicap to theological preaching.

This is not a plea for brief, bright, and breezy inanities. Brevity can disguise shallow thought as well as picture the profound. A simple idea presented by a Simple Simon preacher will not be improved by a brief presentation, except that it will bore the hearer for less time. A profound idea, on the other hand, may be betrayed by much speaking. The congregation is deceived into thinking more is known by the speaker than is really the case. Therefore, let no one think the short sermon is a handicap for its subject if it is properly done. If the short sermon is not shallow, it can hint better than a long one.

The same conclusion can be expressed differently by considering the diversity of the word "truth." Truth has many sides, and each aspect needs to be expressed. However, not all aspects require the same treatment. The verbal media for conveying the different kinds of truth will vary from lengthy discourse to short proverb. History, for instance, requires lengthy presentation. The truth of Presbyterian beginnings will require volumes. To shorten any historical subject may be to deceive. Letters, records, books of the period, secular histories—even artifacts, architecture, art, vestments—all these will play a part in defining the subject. Long manuscripts need to be corrected by long manuscripts so that biases can be balanced. The result is historical truth, defined as well as possible. When historical truth is presented verbally, the form it takes is the lecture or university course.

However, suppose the subject is not history, or English composition, or computer technology, or any other word-intensive subject. Suppose the subject is a relationship, a mystical experience, a feeling, a "you had to be there" type of event. Sometimes a multiplicity of words about this kind of truth withers the embedded vitality. A long essay loses the sense of standing on holy ground. We are apt to say the speaker "doth protest too much."

The subject with which we deal in preaching is the presentation of truth of the second type. The extended language of history and theology is present in a supporting role, and will lend some of the accents. But the essential thing is the truth as it is in Christ Jesus—saving truth, life-changing truth, truth hidden in mystery and yet revealed, truth that may bring both travail and new birth. Words can convey this truth, but the glory must hover about the Holy One of Israel, rather than around the rhetoric. The polished lecture must give way to a sermon in which words assume a sacramental role, conveying grace mysteriously by their presence.

Note how many times in the Bible, when the living God comes close to earth to speak a saving word, the recipient of that word is brought to silence rather than to speech. A classic example is the tumultuous ending of the experience of Job. After Job and his friends have discussed at length the question, "Why do good people suffer?" the God of the universe comes in a whirlwind. All the reasons and disputings get twirled around for the light stuff they are. The response Job makes is an appropriate silence:

> I lay my hand on my mouth.
> I have spoken once, and I will not answer;
> twice, but I will proceed no further. (Job 40:4–5)

There are things to be said, and responses to be made to the experience, but not by those who only think of truth as the accurate description of content subjects.

A minimum or a lack of speech often comes nearer to the point than full-blown verbiage. Thus, lovers may look into each other's eyes and convey much. Thus, the son of F. W. Robertson could fittingly describe his father's character in only one sentence, "My father was real." This may also explain why Jesus gave a "word" of silence to Pilate, and why later, "like a sheep that before its shearers is dumb, so he opened not his mouth" (Isa. 53:7, cf. Acts 8:32). It may also explain why Paul spoke of the foolishness of preaching.

It is almost laughable to suppose that words, any words, can be used to penetrate the saving purpose of God. Paul asks, "Where is the wise man? . . . Where is the debater of this age?" (I Cor. 1:20). The wise of this age are piling up words, and doing it with the cleverness of their professions. We need words that are connected to the Christian faith, words like "Christ and him crucified." The words need to be chosen with care, the sentences fitted with precision, the topic developed with imagination. But, dropped at that point. Dropped knowing that it is impossible to carry those words to their ultimate destination by more words. Only God can do that. The foolishness of preaching is neither to extend speech nor the opposite, to mouth some slapdash one-liners. Preaching must say it, and stop, and let God be God.

T. S. Eliot, in "East Coker," described his own plight as a poet, trying to put into words those meanings which constantly elude words. He called the various forays into his subject "a raid on the inarticulate." According to Eliot, poets fight to recover lost meaning, snatching some only to have it escape. The effort goes on, one engagement after another, but none ends in total victory. All the forays can be judged failures. And yet the effort must be made. Poets feel a compulsion, whether from themselves or from the mysterious truth that eludes them. They must keep on, accepting responsibility for the struggle with words, but not for the effect of the "finished" product. As Eliot concludes:

> For us, there is only the trying.
> The rest is not our business.[13]

Preachers know this same struggle with words, and realize the inadequacy of words. Yet, to use the best words, and to keep trying for the just-right words, that is the aim. The rest is not our business.

Therefore, it is not enough to insist on telling the truth in the pulpit. It is important to identify what kind of truth you want to convey. If it is the truth of Biblical history, Biblical archaeology, New Testament ethics, Old Testament cultic rites, then, of course, the long form is necessary. It is likewise necessary if the sermon is a critique of a movie or the proposal of a new social program. The sermon becomes the lecture. As a lecture that aims to "cover" the subject, the sermon will vary in length with the size of the subject. Perhaps thirty minutes or an hour will not be enough time to present the material. However, with some amount of words in some length of time it will be possible to touch all the boundaries until the subject is well defined and explored. The preacher usually is not interested in truth that has only this linear dimension. This kind of truth, important though it may be, has its place in the Sunday school class, discussion group, or college elective course. On the other hand, the minister's truth is that of personal relationships, of revelation, of saving contact with God, of insight into God's ways with us. The boundaries of this truth always trail off into mystery and elude the very words that give them any shape at all. When the sermon is effective, the listeners identify the kingdom that has been expecting their return for years. The eternal becomes the rock on which to stand, or the compass that directs, or the manna which on that day gives strength.

In other words, the truth of insight, rather than of information, is the aim of the sermon. Insight comes in flash points through the use of an unusual phrase or the intrusion of a life-giving idea. Somehow, by a combination of words and Spirit, an ordinary bush starts to glow and listeners who look in that direction sense that they are on holy ground. This is the promise of the sermon. The mystery of the sermon event is enough within the power of preachers that they give it the best of intellect and preparation. Yet the mystery remains mystery and is always enough out of human control that God remains the sovereign God who reveals himself whenever and to whomever he pleases.

What is the relation between sermon length and the kind of truth that the sermon presents? From one point of view, none at all. God can speak his saving word through many words or few. However, there is in ministers, particularly in mainline denominations, a built-in bias toward scholarly sermons that order the arguments, and encompass the subject, and go on at length, forgetting all the while that the argument has too many strainer holes to carry the divine. A short sermon, on the other hand, can be a confession of faith by its very style. Obviously it cannot convey much information. It makes no attempt to do so. It confesses inadequacy before the fullness of God. Yet it knows that five loaves and two fishes' worth of words can be touched and multiplied and made to feed thousands. This is the miracle ministers wait for once they develop the faith to make small verbal offerings each week and let God be God.

Interestingly enough, the conclusion of this line of theological thinking accords with the time we live in. We began by observing that modern Americans are short of time. They want their message writ large so they can read it on the run. In particular, they are leery of the organized church, and they carry in their minds the stereotype of ministers as pictured in *New Yorker* cartoons. These observations point to brevity in all pulpit work. And yet, if these theological observations we have made are correct, the call for brevity comes from the Biblical revelation too. The mood of the times and theology itself combine to give a united message. They invite ministers to tend to this one aspect of the message—the length of its presentation.

3

CONTAGIOUS COMMUNICATION
UTILIZES BREVITY

There is a third and practical reason for briefer sermons. They communicate better to a modern congregation than do longer sermons, and that because of an intangible force that permeates them. I call this "heat" or passionate intensity. To speak within time limits like a radio announcer, who must stop when the red light comes on, or like a lover on a long-distance call, intensifies the message. It forces the speaker to compress. Heat! Enthusiasm! Aliveness! Too much to say, and too little time in which to say it. These qualities leave their mark on the preacher, and the mark is a plus. Contagious communication! The same force that drives the speaker to brevity also drives the message home. Better communication takes place.

Some speakers convey this excitement in whatever they say, however long it takes to say it. Fidel Castro speaks with excitement for hours. Favorite college professors manage it. Mark Twain did it instinctively. He commented somewhere, "I was born excited." Yet, the odds are against combining duration and intensity. When you have all day to do a simple job, you dawdle. But when the schedule is tight, you snap to. Long sermons invite dawdling. The preacher is encouraged to make points and subpoints, to trace bypaths, amble, pause, and amble again. Long sermons are a temptation to sluggishness, slow pacing, too many digressions. Particularly is this true when the preacher faces first of all a twenty-five-minute time slot rather than a vast and exciting topic. When a long time slot is the first consideration, we are tempted to forage for suitable material. But reverse this. Having found a vast topic, vital to faith, force the topic down to fit a ten- or fifteen-minute time slot. Use economy of language, picturesque phrases, short sentences, rapid transitions, a rough-cast ending. The discipline of doing this works a communication miracle. Passionate intensity, that sleeping giant of good communication, is finally aroused.

Listen to recent masters of brief communication: Harry Reasoner, Howard K. Smith, Rod MacLeish, David Brinkley, or Barbara Walters. First of all, distinguish them from detergent peddlers and people who sell cars. Both operate in seconds of time, but with a difference. The sellers on television say it without having much to say. They rely on gimmicks. They rev up the emotions, add a few jingles, bring on a show-and-tell. Despite all this, most in the audience head for the refrigerator. On the other hand, the masters of quick communication chip away at a mass of important material until a main idea stands out. These speakers do not rant. But the control they exercise leads to intensity, leads to communication.

The problem for preachers is not only to find significant material, Biblical and contemporary, and organize it into a sermon. The added problem is how to compact it before delivery. Whenever a minute of time is spared, or a shaft of illustration replaces a well-developed story, or a change of wording is made toward a leaner and more concise idiom, or a needless bypath is eliminated, the compacting process goes forward. To put wide-ranging thought, amply illustrated, through a tiny time slot and out to a congregation is like moving a king-size bed up a narrow stairway. The project frustrates. It calls for experiment. First this way, then that. Then pondering, planning. Try again. Just so, preachers work with heavy units of thought, phrase blocks, and paragraph progressions, which must be toted into areas and moved into place with endless adjustment.

Whether or not every piece of the sermon fits into the allowable space, the process itself generates heat, that intangible factor of good communication, and the witnesses to its presence and power are all around. As one of the elementary laws of physics states quite simply, to compress is to warm. Fill a bicycle tire with a hand pump and feel the pump, how hot it is. The law of physics is vindicated. Or take a classical witness. The early Hindu scriptures, called Vedas, discuss the creation of the world. The Hindus believed that the raw materials were earth, air, fire, and water. However, they added a fifth factor, called in the Sanskrit *tapas,* or heat. There can be no creation without heat. The Hindu poets take the idea further. In their later scriptures, called the Upanishads, the word *tapas* becomes a synonym for asceticism. What better illustration of a total life lived under compression than a Hindu ascetic? All material accretions and frivolous desires have been stripped away in the quest for enlightenment. The former "rich man" is proceeding through the eye of a needle, and heat is generated in the process. Any stringency, any discipline, any compression aimed at a new creation, produces heat.

These observations are important for our thesis because there is a definite connection in the speaking arts between compression, heat, and communication. Leaving the laws of physics and Hindu mysticism, let us bring into view some illustrations closer to the communication process.

Many creative people testify to this phenomenon of heat. James Baldwin describes his repeated experience in producing an article. He sits, his mind boggled by the task—too many ideas defying too few pages. He thrusts back the chair, paces the room. The frustration mounts. He snaps a pencil in two, kicks the wastebasket, pounds fist in palm, then sits again. The energy builds. The words come into focus. The idea is delivered . . . *The Fire Next Time.* [14] The same experience repeats itself in all the arts. Michelangelo faces a block of marble that others have rejected as too small. Suddenly, after careful sketching, the chips fly like snow, and a figure is delivered. Van Gogh agonizes over sunflowers; Monet over water lilies. Ravel ponders a piano composition, later to become a masterpiece, that in its inception is limited by the fact that his virtuoso friend has only one arm, a left arm at that. In each case, there is some tie between the limited medium, the heat of the creator, and the power of communication.

The law of physics, "to compress is to heat," is thus a law of the novelist, the artist, the musician—and it certainly is a law of rhetoric. Call it enthusiasm, intensity, charisma, forceful speech power. Call it heat. Something hovers around words put under pressure which becomes part of the preacher and which leaps from the pulpit to carry the message through to the congregation. Words forced through the channel of brevity kindle a response at the receiving end—at least attention, if not positive reception. Jesus spanned large areas of Old Testament Scripture in explaining the necessity of the crucifixion. He did it within the time it takes to walk the road to Emmaus. The testimony of the two who listened as they reflected on his words was this: "Did not our hearts burn within us . . ." (Luke 24:32).

Yet the compacting process that is involved in creating short sermons is not necessarily equated with frenzy. In this regard, James Baldwin need not be the model for the sermonizer. Though artists and writers testify to the anguish of preparation, not all kick their wastebaskets. Two analogies, both from the Orient, portray the fire in a slightly different way. I watched a black belt master break five cement blocks, stacked one on top of the other, all resting on two low piers. An untrained Atlas would approach this without preparation. He would proceed like the boy at a carnival who, trying to impress a girl, grabs the mallet, pounds the target, and hopes to ring the bell. Not the karate master. He sat in the lotus position before the five blocks for fifteen minutes. His breathing became deep and measured. His eyes were half closed in meditation. He pondered the material, thought his way through the blocks from top to bottom, collected his energy. Suddenly everything about him came alive. With eyes open, muscles flexed, he quickly bounded with a cry and a chop. A crack ran down the width of the blocks. Mission accomplished.

Similar to the karate master is the Zen artist. The end product will be black strokes on rice paper: perhaps calligraphy, perhaps the form of a lion or an owl. The actual production is surprisingly quick: dashed off, we might say. Yet, such a masterful dashing off! The lion is alive. The spirit of the animal is there, ready to lunge. Similarly, the characters of the calligraphy have a grace and beauty beyond the meaning of the word itself. The Zen artist conveys intensity or grace through work quickly done. The secret, again, is in the preparation. This took days, if not years. Like the karate master before blocks, the artist thinks his way into the lion. In a sense, he becomes the lion. The spirit is caught which in turn catches others who view it on rice paper. Days of brooding, minutes of production. Intensity is caught in the artist's personality and transferred to the viewer.

These analogies characterize the preacher's fire or *tapas*. In preparing, he or she rages like James Baldwin or meditates like a Zen artist. The puzzlement is both the message and the medium. How can you put the vastness of the eternal into the tin cup of words—any words? That in itself is baffling, even if the words are endlessly strung out. It is like putting the ocean into a lake and the lake into a demitasse. Can the revelation be expressed in a short sermon? Can the miracle occur and the Christian koan be cracked? These questions face ministers every time they preach a short sermon. But the effort creates intensity, which aids communication. Listeners listen when fire heats the material. They sense the struggle that went into simplicity.

Three reasons, then, conspire to make the case for brevity. The mood of the times demands it; theology sanctions it; and effective communication utilizes it. However, preaching briefly is not easy. The art has some rules all its own. In Part II, I am going to suggest ten guidelines for preaching briefly. The number is not absolute, and the rules may be considered as suggestions rather than *ex cathedra* pronouncements. First, however, consider a parable rooted in our history.

To what shall we liken the present generation, and with what kind of message shall we come?

It happened that in the midst of a great war, the governor of a certain state proposed to dedicate a cemetery. It was to receive and honor those who had died in a recent battle there. "Whom shall we invite to come, and whom shall we invite to speak?" the governor asked his counselors. All agreed that the statesmen of the nation should attend, the Senators and Congressmen, the governors of nearby states, powerful political figures, the wives of these, and of course, the President of the country. However, it was not easy to determine who should speak.

"Let the President of the country bring the main address," said one member of the committee. "That seems the normal thing to do." The other counselors looked at one another, then up to the ceiling, then down to the floor. Everyone shuffled in an uneasy silence. The governor spoke for the majority. "Hiram, I am not sure the President is the right choice. Some heard him recently when he acted the buffoon, and others call him a "Simple Susan." He is a man too lacking in judgment to highlight the important day."

Many names were presented during the meeting, but only one prevailed. He was the country's foremost orator. He had spoken at leading functions for years. His speeches were collected in volumes for preservation and study. One speech alone was so popular that the money collected helped purchase the nation's leading shrine. The orator was old, but vigorous. He wore his honors well. His frame, his white hair, his beautiful voice, his theatrical gestures, were trademarks of his greatness. "Yes," said the governor, "he is the one." "We agree," said the counselors. "Why did we not think of him sooner?" Thus, a letter was dispatched to the orator, who agreed to come, providing that the dedication date could be moved from October to November so that he had more time to prepare.

"But what shall we do with our poor President?" others asked. "Surely he must have some part, if only he does not say too much and say it too poorly and spoil the day." The counselors selected their special agent to invite the President to give "a few appropriate remarks," and to make sure that the word "few" was emphasized. The agent was also to insist that the dedication day was a most solemn occasion. "Perhaps," said the governor, "if we remind him that the day is a serious one, he will leave at home his homespun humor."

The President was no stranger to the grief of the war, nor to the pain the newly created cemetery represented. So, he thought about what he should say. He thought about it under the pressure of other work—battle communiqués that needed attention, visits from sectional politicians who had problems and requests, cabinet meetings, social functions, even personal problems. He constantly battled the ridicule of those who thought him inept. But he bore that grief, and he knew that the day of dedication required fitting words that might capture the feelings of a nation.

The great orator also prepared. He wrote his speech on pages of foolscap, and even sent a finished copy to the President so they would not overlap inadvertently. Then he waited, and the President waited, for the solemn celebration.

When the day arrived, the crowds gathered. Fifteen thousand —some said thirty or fifty thousand—people were on the hillside of the cemetery. The procession from town arrived on foot and on horseback, including representatives of the government, the army and navy, governors of states, mayors of cities, a regiment of troops, hospital corps and telegraph company representatives, the press, fire departments, citizens of the state and nearby states. Many in the crowd had been standing for two hours and would need to stand longer, for the famous orator was an hour late. But by noon the program started. The invocation was given, the band played, the glee club sang, and the famous orator was presented.

The great man stood in silence before a crowd that stretched to limits that would test his voice. Beyond and around were the wheat fields, the meadows, the peach orchards, long slopes of land, and five and seven miles farther the contemplative blue ridge of a low mountain range. His eyes could sweep them as he faced the audience. He had taken note of it in his prepared and rehearsed address. "Overlooking these broad fields now reposing from the labors of the waning year, the mighty mountains dimly towering before us, the graves of our brethren beneath our feet, it is with hesitation that I raise my poor voice to break the eloquent silence of God and nature. But, the duty to which you have called me must be performed; grant me, I pray you, your indulgence and your sympathy." The orator proceeded, "It was appointed by law in Athens," and gave an extended sketch of the manner in which the Greeks cared for their dead who fell in battle. He spoke of the citizens assembled to consecrate the day. "As my eye ranges over the fields whose sods were so lately moistened by the blood of gallant and loyal men, I feel, as never before, how truly it was said of old that it is sweet and becoming to die for one's country."

Our cities would have been trampled in conquest but for "those who sleep beneath our feet," said the orator. He gave an outline of how the war began, traversed decisive features of the three days of battle, drew parallels from European history, and came to his peroration quoting Pericles on dead patriots: "The whole earth is the sepulchre of illustrious men." He had spoken for an hour and fifty-seven minutes.

The orator came to his closing sentence without a faltering voice: "Down to the latest period of recorded time, in the glorious annals of our common country there will be no brighter page than that which relates the battles of this place." It was the effort of his life, and it embodied the perfections of the school of oratory in which he had spent his career. His erect form and sturdy shoulders, his white hair and head flung back at dramatic points, his poise, and chiefly some quality of inside goodheartedness, held most of his audience to him, though many were inwardly yawning and waiting hopefully for the end.

Having read the orator's address beforehand, the President knew when the moment drew near for him to speak. He took out his own manuscript from a coat pocket, put on his steel-bowed glasses, stirred in his chair, looked over the manuscript, and put it back in his pocket. A glee club sang a specially prepared piece. When it was finished, the announcer spoke the words, "Ladies and gentlemen, the President of our Country." The President rose slowly, and when the commotion subsided, he read in a high-pitched and clear-carrying voice his brief and pithy remarks:

Fourscore and seven years ago our fathers brought forth on this continent a new nation, conceived in Liberty . . .

The speech was over almost before it began. A photographer barely got his head under the hood for an exposure. Some were surprised that it should end before the orator had really begun to get his outdoor voice. The speech was so short in comparison to the oration—two minutes as compared to two hours. Yet it caught the mood of the time and the realities of the occasion.

Verily, verily, I say unto you, this man—the President of the country—spoke that day the fitting and enduring word.[15]

PART II

TEN GUIDELINES

FOR

BRIEF PREACHING

1

THINK SMALL

Any decision to embrace brevity as an important factor in preaching does not come easily. Congregations past and present have been conditioned to know how long the sermon should be. Sermons hover around the thirty-minute mark, and the faithful take it for granted. But the norm needs to be challenged. There are other forces pushing for conciseness in speech, and thus for brevity. They arise from the mood of the times, the sanctions of theology, and the need to communicate the gospel more effectively. Those who hear this drummer march to a different cadence. Their attitude is shaped by the dictum: Think small. They write it large, and accept it as a desirable and self-imposed restraint.

Without this attitude firmly in place, preachers who shorten the sermon will think they have sold out for a mess of pottage. The great preachers of yesterday would not dabble in brevity. They preached long sermons, and included a good deal of solid material. If we turn our backs on this fact, and deliberately craft our proclamation to a shorter time frame, we fly in the face of a venerable tradition. If our attitude of thinking small is not a free choice from deep conviction, we open ourselves to a great amount of self-criticism. On the other hand, if we realize that new occasions teach new duties, then we can accept a new attitude and allow it to permeate the sermonizing process.

To undergird the new conviction, here are a few reminders tossed out at random:

Reminder: Advertisers get a lot of mileage out of spot announcements and flashed on symbols. Men and women in advertising are paid large sums to compress. The effectiveness of a typical Volkswagen ad is a punchy saying, a dominant illustration, and lots of vacant space. The message conveyed depends upon what is *not* said for its full effect.

Reminder: Consult your own experience. Recall a time when you have been on the receiving end of spoken communication. Have you ever heard something that affected you deeply? Was it only a brief conversation? A few sentences heard while turning the radio dial? Or something discussed over coffee? Did the shortness of the message reduce its power? A Latin phrase, *solvitur ambulando*—"it is solved by walking"—was dropped into my mind by a professor at a time when I was quite perplexed. It has stayed with me for years, whereas his lectures, I fear, never lasted beyond the trolley ride home.

Reminder: Again, consult your experience. This time try to remember a lecture or a long sermon that everyone agreed was excellent. What exactly do you remember about it? The single point? The title? Or, simply the emotions it conjured up? Chances are that a major idea or two, surrounded by a positive feeling, is the best you will muster. Those who heard Russell Conwell give his famous lecture "Acres of Diamonds" probably remembered no more than to start looking in their own backyard for things they had dreamed of finding elsewhere, that and a couple of illustrations. The same point could be made as forcefully today in ten minutes as in the hour and more he needed in the nineteenth century.

Reminder: Examine a Zen painting of a lion, or geese, or a bird perched on a bamboo shoot. Black ink on rice paper. Inevitably, a great amount of space is left around the main object. It is not vacant space, but eloquent space. It helps define the object painted. Then, as you concentrate on the object, note the economy of line and statement. A few strokes depicting the essence of the object makes for the power of the effect.

Reminder: Eric Hoffer writes books that are both slender and profound. One day, he made an observation to a friend of mine.

"If you write a good book, it will contain a memorable line. If it is a great book, it will have a good paragraph. If it is a classic, it may have a great chapter. That, and not much more." Such reasoning helps those who deal in words to admit that not all they present is fit for the gods. There is, of necessity, both wheat and chaff in all formal communication, with the constant need for winnowing. Present the kernel. Let more of the chaff blow away.

Reminder: Take any great section of the Bible, prose or poetry, and try writing it in your own words. Most likely the effort will require the use of more words with less effect. Try describing the creation from chaos to Sabbath—indicating by hints and phrases that space and time, the material world, all of nature and human society, were called into being—and be sure to limit yourself to a short chapter comparable to Genesis 1.

George Orwell took a verse from Ecclesiastes and translated it into the idiom of contemporary bureaucracy. The strong, simple language of the Bible reads:

> Again I saw that under the sun the race is not to the swift, nor the battle to the strong, nor bread to the wise, nor riches to the intelligent, nor favor to the men of skill; but time and chance happen to them all. (Eccl. 9:11)

The modern author, said Orwell, would handle the same thought as follows:

> Objective consideration of contemporary phenomena compels the conclusion that success or failure in competitive activities exhibits no tendency to be commensurate with innate capacity, but that a considerable element of the unpredictable must invariably be taken into account.

The rewrite is no improvement. The words used are bigger but not brighter. They do not hang up pictures in the mind, or drive home meaning. Interestingly, the rewrite is longer than the passage in the Bible and communicates with less force. This observation unlocks one of the secrets of the Bible. Throughout the Bible compression and economy are at work, which we overlook when we take a passage and elongate it by the "rewrite" of our many points and illustrations. The process of preaching often destroys the tastiness of the original.

Think small! Evidence of the effectiveness of the advice is all around. It is even obvious in the way most of us preachers receive our inspirations. They do not usually come to us full blown and extensively developed. Mozart's ability to conceive a full and complete musical score while riding in a carriage, and then to set it all down in order at the end of the ride is not the gift of many. Most of us receive an insight into life that is a small but valid testimony to reality. It is just one inspiration that is for real among the billions of already or not yet discovered insights. Keep its identity separate from the multitude around it, and develop it only, so it can be shared and made clear before it evaporates. Do not smother it in the process of describing it, and do not relate it to so many things that its own significance is lost.

Consider how often listeners pick out short sections, even short sayings, from long addresses, leaving the rest as disposable pulp and rind. The embellishments, the long illustrations, the many numbered points, were not needed. They probably detracted. If speeches could focus on their essential points and treat them with an economy of words, they would probably say more to hearers, who do not remember great gobs of material. We feel we must speak long "to get the point across," when the opposite may be true. Listeners remember small amounts. Therefore, preachers should learn to think small confidently, and apply it to the work of producing a sermon.

Jesus himself was the master of thinking small. He spoke about a mustard seed, a pearl, a sparrow, a cup of cold water. Consider the lilies. Look at the woman throwing the mite into the Temple treasury. A certain man went down from Jerusalem to Jericho. A certain woman hid leaven in three measures of meal. These are small flashes, kept small for the sake of clarity and remembered thereby. The vignettes of teaching are not expanded beyond what is needed. That style comprises their charm and effect.

The brevity of Jesus has another aspect. His public teaching is an example of thinking that is intensive rather than extensive. He did not say much about women's rights, or the Palestinian economy, or labor legislation. Abortion, civil rights, ecology, and conservation were not his topics. There was no field which interests us today, or which would have been timely in his own day, that he dealt with exhaustively. He "covered" nothing. And yet he saw deeply into everything. His insights and his salvation are for all seasons. He is therefore the model for preachers who attempt to speak the same kind of saving word. They, too, do not cover any subject, and would not even if they had the time and the competence. They wish to examine small segments appreciatively. They put the pause on the rapid motion picture, and hold the gaze on one part of the whole long enough to say, "Just look at this, will you?"

The short sermon must aim at intensiveness. It has no time to be exhaustive. It cannot relate its findings to the entire range of Christian truth. It can only find a single point that might otherwise be lost, and play with it for a few moments. Little happenings, which might end up as illustrations in a longer sermon, useful and then lost, become the theme of shorter sermons. These almost unnoticed events or ideas are expanded just enough to become memorable. The zoom lens is upon them. The unnoticed becomes visible. Dull listeners become seers and are more apt to see because the preacher is brief and they are in a hurry.

Think small. With this attitude secured, together with the other background assumptions, let us proceed with the second guideline for preaching better by preaching briefly.

2
ADOPT A POETRY MODEL

Sermons are related to poems, and this fact encourages brevity—the type of brevity that communicates with emotional force and from mysterious depths. Here we will be principally concerned with the language of poetry, what we have referred to elsewhere as hinting speech. This language is what gives the sermon its unusual dimension. However, something might also be said for the form of poetry as related to sermons. Poems are bound in certain forms—rhyme, meter, stanza—and, in a sense, so are sermons. So, too, are the Scriptures from which sermons come. For instance, there are many famous refrains in the Bible that mark the progression of thought: Genesis 1 moves with the familiar, "And there was evening and there was morning" of the first (second, third . . .) day, "and God saw that it was good"; Amos scans the borders of Palestine and opens his prophecy with a stanza-by-stanza blast, "For three transgressions of Damascus [Gaza, Tyre, Edom . . .] and for four, I will not turn away the punishment thereof." All the psalms have the stanza quality, with the most vivid being the acrostic structure of Psalm 119, where each stanza begins with a new and successive letter of the Hebrew alphabet, and each line within a given stanza begins with the same Hebrew letter. Just so, there are the balanced lines of the proverbs, the laments, the Beatitudes, the descriptions of trumpets and bowls and seals of the Apocalypse. All of these have a stanza-like quality, and the wording of the stanzas fits a certain pattern.

These are the surface marks of poems, but they do act as channels through which the words must flow. Any structure an author accepts—the sonnet or the epic, for example—is both a limitation and a discipline. If the verbal space is small, like the fourteen lines of a sonnet, every word must be chiseled to fit. The seventeen syllables of a Japanese haiku are even more demanding, and yet able to express phenomenal amounts of fact and surprises of insight. The author decides on the form, and compresses the thought within the form.

We don't usually think of the sermon as a series of stanzas, and yet those who sermonize every week know how much the two or three points get developed with structural sameness. The stereotype of three points and a poem is a stereotype because that is the way the sermon turned out week after week. Even the pulpit greats gave a certain unvarying form to their sermons. Harry Emerson Fosdick always stated his purpose by the second paragraph. Frederick W. Robertson nearly always balanced two main points opposite each other. Peter Marshall's sermons in print had the look of blank verse stanzas. And, whatever your particular form, if you preach regularly, most of your sermons have the same development and style even though the subject matter may differ. The points of the sermon may even have an unconscious sameness of duration, where the total number of minutes is twenty or twenty-five, set by a "clock" hidden somewhere in the intuition.

Now, there is nothing wrong in such a structure. We have managed to fit our words and thoughts into these stanza frames. However, why not experiment with shorter stanzas that will require even more discipline to get the just-right word, with allusions replacing discourses, and one-line illustrations and metaphors doing the work of full-blown stories? If Byron could move from the epic *Childe Harold's Pilgrimage,* a long work, to the much shorter autobiographical poem "On This Day I Complete My Thirty-sixth Year," and if Auden could write the long Christmas oratorio *For the Time Being* and also frame a short tribute "In Memory of W. B. Yeats," surely ministers can move from two or three "stanzas," totaling twenty-five minutes, to the same number of "stanzas," or less, totaling only ten or fifteen minutes. What you select at the start as the form in which to operate will control the manner and form of saying it. And, as in poetry, the briefer the "space" through which the words must flow, the greater the intensity of the thought that comes through to the hearer.

However, if the speaking space is limited, then more than ever the words must be selected with care and precision. This elementary fact is taken for granted by poets. It is a trademark of the profession. Why not also a trademark of the preacher's craft? Consider two stanzas from A. E. Housman, and a few of the comments made about it by Donald Stauffer, formerly chairman of the English Department of Princeton University.[16]

> Into my heart an air that kills
> From yon far country blows:
> What are those blue remembered hills,
> What spires, what farms are those?

> That is the land of lost content,
> I see it shining plain,
> The happy highways where I went
> And cannot come again.

Stauffer comments that no word of this poem can be changed without changing the effect of the whole. The slightly archaic word "yon" brings forcefully to mind the past which underlies the present, and which will add to the pathos of the final line. There is also the concrete action of pointing which "yon" gives. Therefore, the phrase "yon far country" would not be the same as the similar phrase, "distant country." Look at some other word choices. Literally, air does not "kill." And air that "chills" would be more accurate. But, Housman's intuition of a past that cannot return has an intensity that the word "chills" doesn't quite pack. Furthermore, the "spires" in those remembered hills are not just part of the landscape. They also have a connotation of aspiration which belongs to the past and which is often lost in the process of growing old.

Every word of this poem could be picked up, looked at, put back in place, or set aside. The poet himself had to do this. He had to convey intellectual content and insight as to what it means to grow old, plus an emotional intensity about that fact. To this end, every word had to carry its weight of meaning. That is the hard work of being a poet, and it is suggestive of the hard work of being a preacher. As Mark Twain said, the difference between the right word and the almost right word is the difference between lightning and the lightning bug. The work to find the right word, particularly for short sermons, is one small part of the burden of the Lord. We win a hearing for the Word of God through the continual struggle and search for the just-right word.

Housman's poem presents a stabbing intuition, easily recognized by any middle-aged person, even if he or she was never able to put it into language. That intuition, if picked up by the reader with the same intensity with which it was written, might be characterized by the theological terms "event" or "moment." Something has struck home, conveyed by eight well-worded lines that clarified and perhaps brought life. The poem was not simply an illustration of a general truth—that middle-aged people often long for an unrecoverable youth—as if that was the important thing. No. The poem is itself the truth, woven as it is with fact, suggestion, and emotion. The general truth is so woven into the specific wording of the poem as to be inseparable from it. That, too, is the mark of a sermon. The words of it, the Bible teaching, the experience of the minister, fuse in a sermon to produce the mini-revelations God is forever producing through the "foolishness of what we preach."

Consider another interesting quality in the language of poetry which also holds true for sermon language. This quality makes brevity possible, even though it does not necessitate it. I refer to the multidirectional nature of metaphors. The metaphors used by poets and preachers travel in several different realms at the same time. While a word might have a primary use to designate a specific item in one familiar field, it might at the same time have a bundle of hidden meanings in other areas. The word "bug," for instance, might refer to the insect which crawls on my light bulb, and it may also refer to something gnawing at my innards. I am "bugged" by something. At the same time, that very same word might refer to a certain auto crawling along the street, or to a device planted on a vase at the embassy. Depending on the context, the word "bug" can have a primary referent while at the same time hinting at other meanings. The other meanings are not spelled out with exactness, else the power of the original is neutralized.

In a similar way, Biblical words are often supercharged with meaning. A word can have its primary reference to an object in space and time, while also connoting some aspect of the eternal realm. Think for a moment of the word "darkness," which can refer to both a condition of the earth and a condition of the spirit. Compare the meanings of the opposite word, "light." Both darkness and light come through with many different shades of meaning and give excitement to the person who uses them. When the writer of Exodus records the plague of darkness, he says without any further elaboration, "The people of Israel had light where they dwelt" (Ex. 10:23). Immediately, and almost because of the absence of elaboration, we are struck with the double dimension of light and darkness. Their candles were lit, and the God of light was near. John also plays the same game. Judas, having betrayed Jesus, went out, and John simply records: "It was night" (John 13:30). There is no need to comment on the spiritual condition of Judas' soul. When the Gospels describe the crucifixion, they note: "Now from the sixth hour there was darkness over all the land until the ninth hour" (Matt. 27:45). Darkness has every meaning from the sin of man to the subterranean depths of the underworld, from the chaotic darkness before creation to the darkness of city streets where crime breeds and hatches. The word is both precise and vague, running off into meanings that escape full definition. Perhaps, as Jung suggests, there are images like darkness which permeate the race and can be called out of the depths and identified by being named. However, for those in the Judeo-Christian tradition, there are countless associations which can be alluded to by words, which constantly travel in several dimensions at the same time: words like kingdom, water, birth, city, tree, fruit, garden. All keen users of language know this complexity of metaphorical words and capitalize on it. When Othello has determined to kill Desdemona and arrives to do the deed, the famous line he speaks is: "Put out the light, and then put out the light."

What does this have to do with brevity? Much in every way. Words that travel in many dimensions have power to the degree that their many meanings are not spelled out in detail. They are left with the strange quality of specific vagueness. As Jonathan Price comments, Shakespeare ruminates on life's mysteries in *King Lear* and concludes solemnly, "Ripeness is all." But what is ripeness? Price notes that it is one of the most suggestive, but least definite words going. He himself tried to come up with equivalents for the phrase "Ripeness is all," and ended with a baker's dozen, but none of them would do. He says, "Think of how much more limiting each would have been: timing is all, the moment is all, maturity is all, lush fruit is all—no, the most powerful word is the one which escapes such easy 'answers.' "[17] Just so with many statements of Scripture or sermon, the extended meanings do not help. Unraveling the ambiguity of deliberately chosen words like "new birth" may have the unwanted result of robbing the phrase of its power.

Similarly, the overuse, even of a fitting word, dribbles away its power. Price observes that a demagogue's slogan, such as "law 'n' order," gets sounded so often that it finally declines into a joke which blows away in irony and then mocks the maker. Preachers often get trapped into a pattern of vain repetition so that the phrases become trite and the message easy to ignore. The phrases may be religious, as when an evangelist asks, "Are you blood-bought and heaven-bound?"; or they may be common banalities like "nitty-gritty," "meaningful," "bottom line." The first person who described the "nitty-gritty" may have been saying something original. The hundredth person who repeated it had simply run out of significant vocabulary. The same is true of words used to bless or curse, where the vocabulary does not have the freshness of a poet's flair.

Avoid the overuse of significant words. Avoid the full-drawn explanation of significant words. Let the ambiguities have their full effect. Work for the right words which carry the right emotions and connotations. Shape them and fit them as a poet chooses words for a sonnet. Fit them into smaller spaces, deliberately fashioning "stanzas" that require less time/space than normal. That is, adopt a poetry model in the preparation of sermons.

3

SELECT A SIMPLE UNITY

Every sermon needs a unifying idea before the first sentence is written. If there is no goal, then one road is as good as another to get there. Shortness without a unity only means less tedium, not better preaching. There must be a single clear purpose around which to build the introduction and conclusion and all points in between. There is nothing startling in this observation. What is sometimes forgotten is that unity comes in different sizes. For a short sermon, select a simple unity.

When Rembrandt decided to paint a canvas showing the whole of Matthew 19, he accomplished the feat. All the characters are there: the sick, the Pharisees, the child, the rich young ruler, Jesus. Furthermore, the unity is there as well. The eye travels to the Master among the swarm of figures depicted. However, the picture does not represent a simple unity. It has a cast of thousands, united by the central figure of Jesus.

For a simple unity, consider Rembrandt's more famous *Descent from the Cross.* In this picture, Jesus is again central. You feel this by the gaze of the few involved, by the shadings which move from near solid brown at the periphery to incandescent white at the center. However, the unity is simpler, easier to spot, more important. Brevity demands this type of unity. It has no time to choreograph the cast of thousands. It wants to sketch one thing boldly, so that someone walking through the gallery enroute to the back door can still catch the meaning.

Let us now apply this insight to the sermon. In particular, we will consider some sermon possibilities in the Book of Jonah. This book has some built-in advantages in that the story itself has a unity. Yet the same story can be tilted in different directions, depending on the problem to be addressed. One legitimate theme would be: "There is no hiding place from God." This theme would certainly focus on the first two chapters, where the prophet tries to run away and is caught. A parallel passage could be found in the Psalms: "If I take the wings of the morning and dwell in the uttermost parts of the sea, even there thy hand shall lead me" (Ps. 139:9–10). In this theme, the merciful pursuit of God could be stressed. God is the "Hound of heaven," who is merciful despite the scary circumstances that often surround the pursued. On the other hand, and with a very slight tilt to the same idea, a more somber thought could be developed. This one would take the form, "Be sure your sin will find you out." This theme will portray the storm and the fish as judgment. Perhaps both ideas could be developed in one sermon, though a short sermon would probably pick up only one of these two for its main idea.

But there is far more than this in Jonah. A third theme, and one closer to the New Testament, is the possibility of a second chance, even after you have badly missed the will of God. A text for this approach could be Jonah 3:1: "The word of the LORD came to Jonah *a second time.*" The title for this text could be, "There's Hope When You Miss Your Calling." It would allow for some discussion of resurrection and contemporary experience. In the story, the resurrection happens out of the depths, when destruction is overcome by the power of God. This possibility is worth a sermon, but not the same sermon as the other two.

A fourth sermon possibility might be entitled, "A Pinprick to Provincialism." This theme is probably closer to the real intent of the author than any of these previously mentioned. Apparently, postexilic Jews, disgusted with far-off places and rough treatment by world powers, decided to retrench to the hills of Judah. They had enough of exile in Babylon. Now was the time to "hole in," far from the madding crowd. They were becoming a people of the Book, fiercely isolationist in mentality. The Book of Jonah is a protest against this attitude. This author sees the word of the Lord pointing to Nineveh and far-off horizons. Because of this, the book can apply to postexilic Judaism or post-Vietnam American Christianity. Provincialism always plagues the people of God. Thus, the Book of Jonah addresses a contemporary problem. To pick up this unity, the preacher must tilt the story toward the end chapters and allow the New Testament note to be played, that God so loved the world.

A fifth and last sermon unity—though there are others—might come from the humorous, artful finale, the conversion of Nineveh. In this episode, the little Jew Jonah mutters some invective, while God's mercy proceeds to overcome the expected judgment. Nineveh repents. A title like "Don't Give Up on Nineveh" could introduce a sermon on forgiveness. The sermon could stress that God's redemption takes place in the most unlikely places. To accomplish this unity, the tilt would be toward chapter 4. It would involve a vivid retelling of the story of Jonah, a buildup to a climax in the conversion of Nineveh, and the repetition of the theme as a conclusion. This and not much more is needed for any who choose this topic.

Thus, at least five possibilities exist in one short book. A choice must be made as to which will be the basis for the particular sermon. The emphasis falls in different places. Without this prior choice of a simple unity, the end product will be a muddy combination or an intricate discourse without movement and destination.

4
STAY CLOSE TO THE ORIGINAL INSPIRATION

The birth of ideas, Biblical or otherwise, is as mysterious as all other births. The source is elusive, even though the testimony to its having occurred is persistent and verifiable. The thought for a sermon strikes out of the blue, seemingly from nowhere. In fact, even secular people have sensed the uncanny, almost divine nature of origins. Nietzsche, no friend of Christianity, in observing the upsurge of his own ideas, commented, "One can hardly reject completely the idea that one is the mere incarnation, or mouthpiece, or medium of some almighty power."[18] However, once the visitation has occurred, as in the case of a given sermon idea, what is it that is given?

Inevitably, it is a single insight, taken from your known experience and Biblical study, that becomes supercharged with a relevant meaning. The single idea may promise a dozen connections to your other knowledge. The idea itself may be in great need of further thought and elucidation. Sometimes it is no more than the pressure of a divining rod, which old-timers used in the search for underground water. But always, the focus is on one spot that, for some unknown reason, seems to invite a sermon.

We might use the term "revelation" for that weekly experience of preachers. The curtain is drawn back on a specific. Tillich defined revelation as a coming together of a constellation of events: a Scripture, the time we live in, and the experience we bring to both. All three come together in an unusual pattern, and if we are wise, we follow.

Let me sketch a few "constellations" from my own recent experience:

1. The story of Nicodemus (John 3) is so familiar that apparently nothing new can be said. Furthermore, the phrase "new birth" has been used as the loyalty oath of so many fundamentalist groups that it almost makes nonfundamentalists look the other way. One day, however, I was struck by a phrase I had overlooked. Nicodemus' question was not "How can I be born again?" but rather "How can a man be born *when he is old?*" Here is a man caught in the aging process, who is worried about the meaning of life, or his ability to do any new thing, or to change directions in any radical way. Anyone over forty will probably identify with his fear of creeping stagnation, and the nostalgia for that pioneer thinking and acting he or she did in college, and the grim thought that maybe there is nothing ahead of any significance. Is this the period of life when we must sorrowfully acknowledge that "the same wheel deepens the same rut year after year"?

"When he is old" is the singular point of a revelation from a story that might otherwise fade off in vague familiarity. I knew the story generally and had some reason to identify with Nicodemus' question. I am a middle-aged man and have normal feelings of middle age. But certain other factors were also whirring about. Gail Sheehy's *Passages* was in my mind. I had attended a meeting and heard someone read the Nicodemus story, stumbling over the phrase "when he is old." To fumble a reading is not normally helpful. In this case it emphasized the forgotten phrase. These, then, were the parts of the constellation which immediately came together to form the possibility of a sermon. Let me give another illustration.

2. The two accounts of creation, one in Genesis 1 and the other in Genesis 2, had always interested me as a critical and scholarly problem, but not as a homiletical opportunity. Much use and misuse has been made of these stories, sometimes in order to make them conform to the latest scientific discoveries, at other times in order to refute the premise of evolution. One day, a homiletical idea struck that took advantage of scholarly

findings without entering into the science-and-the-Bible thicket. Suppose the editors who allowed two different creation stories to stand side by side did so not because they slipped up in the use of the blue pencil, but because they wanted to present two quite different views of the human race? Suppose they took this method to emphasize the grandeur and the weakness of us all? In the first poem, man and woman are at the head of creation, surrounded by glory. They are to "have dominion," "subdue," control the universe with only the overarching Deity as the limit. In the second story, man is created first and of the dust of the earth, and woman is united to man, and of the same basic "stuff." In this picture, the human race begins from inert matter, the type of material that we walk on or build on. From this point of view, the possibility of the human race is not in ourselves but in the God who touches us to life. Placing the first and the second view side by side, I found the possibility of a two-point sermon taking shape, after the manner of F. W. Robertson. The Scriptures were once again "speaking to my condition." Sometimes I am on top of the world, and feel the touch of greatness. I am, in the words of the psalmist, "a little lower than the angels" (Psalm 8:5). The psalmist used the word *elohim* for "angels," so the verse really could be translated, "a little lower than God." This is not blasphemy. Some days I do feel this good about my powers. At the other extreme, there are days when I do not need convincing that I am of the dust of the earth. Another psalmist caught this truth when he pictured God holding up his hand like a policeman at an intersection, and saying "Turn back, O children of men!" (Psalm 90:3). That is, turn back to the dust from whence we came. Another psalmist says it more clearly. "He knows our frame; he remembers that we are dust" (Psalm 103:14). Thus the inspiration point for a sermon is the grandeur and weakness of us all, rather than the threadworn God-and-science controversy, which is so often imposed upon Genesis 1 and 2.

3. One more example. A line popped out in a rereading of the account of the Day of Atonement in Leviticus 16. The overall story tells of the preparation of the priest and the two goats—

one for sacrifice and the other as the scapegoat. The solemn celebration of the Day of Atonement is established. However, in the procedural account, this line occurs without embellishment: "So shall [the priest] do for the tent of meeting, which abides with them in the midst of their uncleannesses" (Lev. 16:16). Some further information is needed to complete the picture in this verse. Israel's twelve tribes were moving from Egypt through the desert. Camp was pitched in a large circle, three tribes around each point of the compass. The divine control center was a special tent called the "Tent of Meeting." Where was it situated? At the center. "In the midst of their uncleannesses." This is the Old Testament version of the incarnation, "God with us." It suddenly clicked that in the famous prologue of John's Gospel, where it says, "the Word became flesh and dwelt among us" (John 1:14), the Greek word for "dwelt" comes from *skēnē,* meaning "tent." God has never been a runaway God, or one who pulls his robes up to the cleaner heavens above. Always, he has provided the Tent of Meeting.

Every minister receives this kind of revelation which becomes the revelation point for sermons. However, a few observations are in order. First of all, the revelation points are life-giving. They seem to be in contact with the divine power source and give some specific meanings out of the plethora of vague and general knowledge that is in the mind at any one time. When mini-revelations are given, the Spirit broods over the chaos until a single and identifiable shape appears in enough surrounding light that you can say, "That's good!" This was my experience in the three examples used above, and continues as the weekly touch of life that comes unsolicited through sermonizing.

A second observation. The original impulse which guided the sermon preparation, and which led to points one, two, and three, and a host of explanations and illustrations, was often smothered by overtalk and overthought. Looking back over past sermons, long since thrown into the barrel, I found that the memorable part was still the original impulse somewhat clarified, rather than the layers of meaning with which my sermon embellished it.

This recollection points in the direction of brevity, if for no other reason than for clarity and memorability. The sermon is best when the development is faithful to the original impulse. Otherwise its singularity blends back into the general knowledge from which it was extracted in the first place. It then becomes a classic example of love's labor lost. The extra verbiage and thought merely blunts the effect.

James Cleland relates a parable of the sermon which loses its well-honed shape and purpose.[19] R. D. Whitehorn, principal of Westminster College, Cambridge, once showed him a news clipping about the discovery of an ancient holy ax in Ireland. There was one sentence in the article that made them both chuckle and shudder: "The sacred character of the axe is conjectured from the absence of an effective cutting edge"—an unconscious but valid analysis of much of our preaching. Too blunted.

This blunting seldom occurs in the teaching of the great religious figures of the world. Intuitively they knew the force of directness and brevity. Thus Buddha could relate a parable of the mustard seed, Lao-tzu could utter mystical two-liners, Confucius his apothegms, Japanese Buddhists their koans, Solomon his proverbs, and Jesus the famous parables, logia, and rhythmical sayings. What we remember of any of these leaders is not their intricacies of logic or fine-spun philosophy, but important things they presented briefly. The parables of Jesus, for instance, have one important thing to emphasize, even though they have many overtones. The Beatitudes are memorable not only for thought but also for the balanced phrasing and clipped language. Some scholars believe that the Beatitudes were originally spoken in Aramaic and probably rhymed. The turns of phrase in the sayings of Jesus have the same clipped quality of thought put under pressure, confined to the space of a sentence, made to yield meaning by choice of words or arrangement of words. "Render to Caesar the things that are Caesar's, and to God the things that are God's" (Mark 12:17). "No one who puts his hand to the plow and looks back is fit for the kingdom of God" (Luke 9:62). "Whoever would save his life will lose it; and whoever loses his life for my sake and the gospel's will save it"

(Mark 8:35). "You, therefore, must be perfect, as your heavenly Father is perfect" (Matt. 5:48). "Our Father who art in heaven, hallowed be thy name . . ." (Matt. 6:9). If anyone asks, "What did Jesus teach?" these lines readily come to mind. They have form and content in a graspable way. They would not be improved by extended language.

The original impulse of a revelation points; it is not smothered in too much language. That is the lesson to be learned from Jesus, as well as from the leaders of all world religions. For instance, if you believed and wanted to teach that we are united to nature; that nature is a totality; that we little affect that totality of which we are a part; that a quiet recognition of this is far to be preferred to a frantic running around the world in eighty days, we can say this in a string of phrases such as compose this lengthy and convoluted sentence. However, it would not be as clear to the average listener as the famous Buddhist two-liner:

> Sitting quietly, doing nothing
> Spring comes; the grass grows by itself.

The Buddha, who always protested the blunting effect of verbiage, told a parable of the poisoned arrow. A man shot by a poisoned arrow falls to the ground. Crowds gather. One man in the crowd looks and says, "I wonder who shot the arrow?" Another builds on that by estimating the direction from which the arrow was shot and the distance of the archer from the body. A third gets into the act by raising the question as to what kind of poison was used. Buddha then brought the point home. "Why don't you stop talking and pull out the arrow?" Precisely.

We have already commented on the damage that succeeding generations do to the vital sayings of the masters. New followers try to make the original meaning so precise that no deviation can occur, no heresy be promoted. The result is lawyers' language, the extension of paraphrases, concern with the minutiae, and the loss of forceful and brief presentation. Spontaneity and freedom depart, and much of the deep seeing as well. In the process of spelling out all the details the original inspiration gets "sicklied o'er with the pale cast of thought," and multidimensional language gets flattened out and elongated.

Creative epochs are followed by some form of scholasticism which kills the many-splendored thing. Jesus, who wrote nothing, but whose thoughts could stick and grow like seeds in soil, is followed by the ecumenical councils, which could fight over a diphthong. The Reformers of the sixteenth century are followed by the scholastics of the seventeenth. Karl Barth breaks new ground in *The Epistle to the Romans,* but along come the Barthians. The movement seems inevitable, perhaps conditioned by the pendulum swing of history. However, the end result of scholasticism is the same: an increase of language, an attempt to imprison thought in logic, a weariness to those who want to learn, and a movement toward the death of the original impulse.

Fortunately for preachers, these are not scholastic days. The mood is against attempts to tie religious thought in neat bundles. The "proofs" for God, defense of miracles, systematics—all the stock-in-trade of theology which rested upon the *tour de force* of reason—all these have shown up poorly dressed for today's occasion. The times call for the same insight and clarity of language that existed in the original revelation. The overtalk surrounding the creative insight is a detriment to the insight.

Preachers, therefore, should exercise their power of choice as they scan the options for presenting their message. Historically, the message began as a creative impulse, fresh and incisive, and slowly went downhill into scholasticism. When preachers overdevelop and overargue, they have arrived at the scholastic side of the presentation. Hinting speech, condensed expression, poetic language, rough-hewn endings, are at the opposite side. The closer preaching is to this side of the line, the more it will appeal to modern Americans and get through to the control center where they make their decisions.

Since we have already likened a sermon to a poem, it is interesting to find the same criticism of overstatement made by Donald Stauffer. He writes: "A heavy weight of details does not usually increase the illusion of reality, but rather leads to bewil-

derment. Poems attempting to describe natural objects, a difficult task at all times, most frequently fail because they are
overloaded with data. They stifle us with a ton of feathers."[20]
The relevance of this criticism to discourse other than poems is
clear. The original impulse needs to breathe freely, without
being smothered.

5
MAKE THE POINT QUICKLY

Have unity? Then travel! No delay! Jump right in! Get to it! The opening shows you mean business. Let the major idea stand out clearly from the start. This is part of thinking small. No time to dawdle with anecdotes or an announcement you forgot to make earlier. Once the Scripture ends and a moment's pause has built expectancy, make a dash for the main point. Feel like a sprinter, toe on line, waiting for the opening gun.

At the very start, two temptations prowl the road. One growls, "Be relevant"; the other, "Be Biblical." You must growl even louder, and with more command, "Both relevant and Biblical, and *at the same time.*" If your aim is relevance, as if the Bible were an obstacle to that, you can jump right in with an attention grabber, but the result is more like an editorial than a sermon. Thus you can say: "Ten thousand babies will die from starvation before we go to sleep tonight. Yet we go about our business and accept our meals as if eating and doing were open to everyone." This is an all-right opening that can discuss causes and cures for the problem of world hunger, but the sentences have not necessarily introduced a sermon. Perhaps a good editorial is born, but no "thus saith the Lord."

The other temptation is to explain the Bible in a scholarly, accurate way, without ever dealing with the question, "So what?" Thus, a sermon on the good Samaritan could open as follows, and be just as bad as the non-Biblical one: "Samaritans hated Jews. There was a long tradition behind it. Samaritans probably came into the Palestine scene after the Assyrian invasion. At that time . . ." The sermon would then proceed, discussing the nature of priests and Levites, the topography of the Jericho road, the type of treatment someone would likely receive at an inn. The conclusion would be, "If a Samaritan could love a Jew, we can certainly love the dispossessed, hurting people of earth." The preacher of this sermon took as his task a Biblical explanation of Jesus' parable, tacking on a relevant thought at the close. Meanwhile, the congregation may be mentally mowing lawns and cooking roasts while the preacher is still walking the donkey up to the inn.

A Biblical sermon laces Bible and relevance together without the seam showing. This type of sermon jumps in with the Bible and the contemporary problem superimposed, so that the Word of God is not simply "back there," nor the main point twenty jumps ahead of the ancient tradition. The authority of the sermon from the outset is the statement of the Biblical text with overtones so contemporary that the listeners sense they are being spoken to in the "now." For instance, let us try to combine the two former introductions into the opening of a Biblical sermon: "A priest and a Levite—two religious and busy men— descended in turn the tortuous no-man's-land between Jerusalem and Jericho. Before them was a man, beaten and robbed and needing help. Conveniently, they walked around him, so as to keep their downtown appointments. This sounds calloused, incredible, and slightly overdrawn. Church people doing that? Yet, lying on our road today are ten thousand infants who will starve to death before we sleep. We will pass them by on the other side; not caring; too busy to help; tied to a schedule. The priest and the Levite apparently wear Geneva gowns and gray-flannel suits and their wives are persons of fashion . . ." This sermon could then develop as its theme "The Sin of Not Caring" or "Too Busy with Church Work" or "Love Is Something You Do." Whatever single theme gets the nod, the past is brought up and interlaced with the present.

By contrast, the bad type of introduction mentioned earlier has been described as theological ping-pong. The thought ball moves back and forth between then and now, ancient history and modern times. The net is a string of phrases that mark off the two playing areas: phrases such as "Now what does that mean for today?" or "What would Amos say if he were living outside Washington?" This is bad theology. It is time-consuming and causes the mental neck to ache. The preacher is engaged in a back-and-forth game instead of a simultaneous then-now presentation.

One significant conclusion of Old Testament study is a recognition of how often ancient traditions are retold to a new generation without playing ping-pong. A good example is the story of the exodus as told in Deuteronomy. Casual modern readers interpret this as a second on-the-scene account of the march to the Promised Land. The law is given, the march through the desert is traced, the call for commitment is extended. Yet the writer also relates the story to a more settled and cultured way of life, where people are no longer nomads, and where the problems of civilization and kingship are intruding. The time of writing is at least five hundred years after the original exodus. At this later time a more sophisticated farming society was slipping away from the call of God. The new generation needed to stand at the point of their beginnings and renew the same covenant that bound their ancestors. They had to choose for or against the God of Sinai, just as their fathers had done. In this regard, Deuteronomy functioned much like the television series called *Roots,* which spoke to our American racial situation of the late 1970's in the very act of telling the story of the coming of a slave family to America. For the readers of Deuteronomy, "then" and "now" coalesced. The setting was the exodus, the audience was the nation during the reign of Josiah, a situation centuries later. Yet modern readers scarcely detect the seam that holds these two historic epochs together.

A term used by some scholars for this type of preaching is called "re-presentation." Re-presentation happens in all good Biblical sermons when an ancient story connects with a contemporary problem without the seam showing. The modern overtones come through without being obvious. They are there simply in the way the ancient story is shaped. G. Ernest Wright describes this approach as follows: "We are confronted with the activity of men in whom we see ourselves so that the distance between the Biblical generations is bridged and we become participants in the original history in order to participate rightly in our own."[21]

This line of reasoning—re-presentation rather than ping-pong —applies to the sermon as a whole. Yet the introduction is critical to what follows. If the sermon is to be an editorial, you will know it by the opening. The Biblical note will be absent even if the Bible was read before preaching. If ping-pong is going to be played, the introduction will probably stay in the Bible court for a while before the play gets over the net into modern times. If re-presentation is in mind, the preacher will connect the Bible story with its modern overtones. This is both theologically correct and far less time-consuming.

6
TRIM THE CAST

The unity must be simple, but the entire sermon must be trimmed. Especially in the body of the sermon, the preacher must think small. Imagine you are producing a budget motion picture. Don't hire too many extras. Eliminate the bit parts and subplots. Have a major statement, announce it at the opening, perhaps sound it repeatedly—but think in the style of Ingmar Bergman, not Cecil B. DeMille. The cast of thousands belongs to another era.

The cast of the sermon is varied. Major roles are given to points one, two, and three. These march the unity through a few important ramifications and help toward a denouement. Without these, the unity wouldn't flow, nor would it have variety. Minor roles are given to illustrations. They give the unity concrete shape and visual attractiveness. If one picture is worth a thousand words, the right illustration will shorten as well as drive home the point. Illustrations suggest, make vivid, illumine, even while they keep their status as minor actors. Too many illustrations speaking too long will only upstage the major characters and the central theme. Make them sit down when they have done their work, or else leave them out.

One supporting cast member that is sometimes missed is the refrain. Phrases interspersed throughout the sermon that repeat the theme serve to focus all eyes on the hero. These phrases trip the listener's mind before it wanders. They rivet attention on the reason why the sermon is being preached.

Well and good. Employ a supporting cast, but econo-
mize. The modern congregation does not want to provide an ela-
borate budget. Perhaps there should be two points instead of
three, particularly if they can be counterpoised with the skill
of an F. W. Robertson. Have short illustrations, and not too
many. Use repetition, but sparingly. And forget the poem at the
end. The end of a sermon can be as unfinished as an unresolved
rock number, or as a line sketch used as a model for a fleshed-
out painting.

The use of illustrations presents a particular problem. The
question is not always "how many illustrations?" but "what
kind?" The long sermons of Charles H. Spurgeon had few illustrations. Where they occur in the dense forest of theological
statement, they are like shafts of sunlight in a forest. A deft
illustration will function like this. It has the same proportion as
sunlight streaking through trees. It gives relief and variety and
allows for vision. By it the trees are discerned. Too much illustration and too long an illustration is like sunlight in a clearing.
Where are the shade, the substance, and the timber? Modern
masters such as Leslie Weatherhead, James Stewart, and Ralph
Sockman did strike a balance between substance and light
shafts, but their style of illustrating was broader than is good for
a brief, terse style. Also, some of the nuances are missing which
make for deftness in the late twentieth century. Arthur Gossip,
of the literary preachers, was unusually deft in handling his
illustrations. They are usually depicted with a few light strokes,
enough to catch the significance and to allow the reader's imagination to go to work. However, Gossip was not a brief sermonizer, and his illustrations are usually drawn from classical
literature.

Here are a few suggestions as to the relative value of sermon
illustrations:

—A modern or common story of everyday happenings, told
only in part, rates higher than one well-told story from the
classics.

—An illustration of something that happened since 1970,

stripped of all embellishment, rates higher than one from the New Deal or the Great Society.

—World War II stories and conversions under Billy Sunday or Dwight L. Moody rate close to zero. They drag the tempo and bore the audience.

—Not far from zero is doggerel poetry or favorites from Browning or Rossetti. Even the rhyme and the cadence of the latter two are the step of another century.

—Allusions to stories, particularly those from the daily newspaper or television or the community paper strike deeper than the full telling of them.

—The full telling of a familiar story in a prosaic way rates a minus score.

—The full telling of two stories back to back, illustrating the same point, rates still lower.

Let's go back to the Book of Jonah. If the prophet is described as the Archie Bunker of Judaism, you have pegged him as prejudiced, volatile, and belligerent. Nothing needs to be said about Archie Bunker. You can be sure that the congregation knows even though the show is no longer produced. You do not need to throw in an episode or two from some remembered program. If you did, you'd be preaching on Archie and not on Jonah. The art of allusion rather than the full telling can send shafts of light in a minimum of time. Here is a homemade sample.

> The church, spear in hand, often tilts at windmills. To realists, this seems foolish. A bit part in the Theatre of the Absurd. Will Godot ever come? To the church itself the role is difficult— collectively to pass through the dark night of the soul. Yet, in its persistent clutch on the impossible dream, that church has grasped the one thing in Pandora's box that gives life its luster. Hope! In the absurd clutch on hope, we of the church believe we might yet see the "spires away on the world's rim."

In a few sentences, and without slowing down thought, reference is made to Cervantes' *Don Quixote,* Samuel Beckett's *Waiting for Godot,* John of the Cross and the mystics, Greek mythology, and John Masefield's "The Seekers." The trick is in allusion. Those hearers who know the reference are helped. Those who don't know are not hindered. The pace still moves rapidly.

Fuller stories can be told, if compressed and sharpened. For example, return to Jonah, and the option: "Don't Give Up on Nineveh." When I preached this, a professor friend had just returned from East Germany. He takes a group of local students to this sector every summer, and they visit outstanding political and religious leaders. This year, Dr. Foster brought home an East German newspaper reporting on the Christian-Marxist dialogue. My friend often lectures in universities, at the invitation of East Germans, on the relationship between Christianity and Marxism, particularly as to how both groups see the nature of man, and the possibilities for the future. Therefore he has a professional and a practical knowledge of what is happening behind the iron curtain. The paper described a suburb of Krakow, where the Catholic Church held worship services out-of-doors. On one day, thirteen services were held, each with three to seven thousand in attendance! A Western observer asked the Marxist reporter—and this too was reported—if this did not disprove Marx's contention that religion would soon wither away. The communist replied: "Not really. The real proof of the Marxist doctrine will be revealed in the future, or in the capitalistic West, where the churches are empty." That is great grist for the Jonah sermon, but not all of it. Here is the ending of the Jonah sermon which refers to this news account:

> Nineveh is the place deserving judgment. Its record of abuse is long. By our calculation, judgment is long overdue. But then— and sometimes against our desire—God interjects a merciful surprise, and says, "Don't give up on Nineveh." Recently, a friend gave me a news release from a communist country, part of the "godless Red economic bloc." Outside the city of Krakow, Poland, the paper reported, there is such a turning to God that on one day, thirteen services of Christian worship were held, each with three to seven thousand attending. That is a story from modern Nineveh. We like to feel that Nineveh is ripe for judgment, and that it will never change. Yet, the Spirit of God is at work there. People are repenting there, and they worship. . . .,.

Don't give up on Nineveh. Any Nineveh. Anywhere.

Note that I have not described my friend, how he got the paper, or what he does with his summers, or how we met. Nor did I use the reporter's reference to the Marxist criticism of Western Christianity. This added twist would have been excellent if the text had been, "Judge not, that you be not judged." My sermon's main point was that God's mercy pops up in unexpected places. The full newspaper story would undermine that unity.

7

TIME'S UP—SIGN OFF!

You began with a theme, got into it quickly, developed it with trim variations, illustrated it deftly. Now get out in a hurry. Drop it and run.

The ending of a brief sermon carries its own distinctive trademark. It can be abrupt, without flourishes. Eloquence is underplayed. Gimmicks of rhetoric are avoided. Get to it, do the job, get out in a hurry. Don't say it all or attempt to throw the last rope of thought around a far-off, wandering subject. As long as something worth saying was unified, cut out quickly.

Knowing when the cut-out point is reached is not always easy to determine. One of the modern abstract painters, Jackson Pollock, was asked by a lady how he knew when a painting was finished. He replied with a query, "Madame, how do you know when you have finished making love?" Perhaps knowing the time to end is an art or an intuition, or it is the end of an inspirational surge. More to the point, the time to end is when it makes sense to repeat the opening without committing a tautology.

Let's consider a great sermon by Edmund Steimle, "Address Not Known." Speaking time—about sixteen minutes. Text—Matt. 25:1–13, the parable of the wise and foolish virgins. Here is the opening paragraph:

In W. H. Auden's "Victor, A Ballad," Victor is betrayed by his wife. So . . .

> Victor walked out into the High Street,
>   He walked to the edge of the town;
> He came to the allotments and the rubbish heap;
>   And his tears came tumbling down.
>
> Victor looked up at the sunset
>   As he stood there all alone;
> Cried: "Are you in Heaven, Father?"
>   But the sky said, "Address not known."

> I suppose almost every last one of us has had some experience like that: maybe brought on by a personal crisis as with Victor; maybe through a national crisis like the unending agony in Southeast Asia; maybe simply as a result of the wearing down by the years when prayer seems like talking into an empty barrel. . . . And to our attempts to "find God" somewhere, to listen to his voice, to get some assurance that there really is a "father" up in the sky somewhere, or in the depths of our being, the answer is the same, "Address not known."

Good opening. He has caught a modern mood. Who can't identify with this? Yet, what is the gospel? This soon opens up a surprising twist given to the parable of the virgins. When this old territory is revisited, a new meaning is discovered. Usually, interpreters of this parable stress the any-moment return of Christ. The theme is expectancy. Be ready with your wicks trimmed and your lamps filled with oil, for the bridegroom is coming soon. But Steimle doesn't play upon this theme at all. He stresses the readiness for a long wait, and the need to prepare for it with trimmed wicks and ample fuel. What many Christians take as abnormal, the absence of God over a long period, is more normal than we realize. Be ready for it, Steimle insists. With that explanation, he presents the conclusion of the sermon:

> I suppose it all adds up to whether in the face of the question, "Are you in heaven, Father?" we can take the reply, "Address not known," and hang in there and wait. And if you who are here are here because you are more disturbed by silence, by absence, by delay, then I suspect you are in better shape religiously than those who are not. Or so this parable seems to read.[22]

Note the repetition of the opening. Note, too, the brevity of the conclusion. Yet, the probings in between beginning and end of the sermon, the surprise twist to the parable, the terse illustrations—often one-liners—mean no tautology. A good theme is played, varied, then dropped.

Sermons of the old school seldom did this. They were structured in a classic style and ended gracefully. Balanced opposites handled by Frederick W. Robertson, deep and imaginative theology developed by Phillips Brooks, or the more typical three points and a poem have all done yeoman service. The impression they now convey as you survey the effort from a distance is the questionable virtue of being "nice." High flying, majestic, colorful, but not apt to make anyone salute.

The difference in style of ending—modern as over against classical—is not just in sermons. Parallels exist in the arts. Canvases before the age of Impressionism were like classical sermons, never finished until every last part of the picture, every brush stroke, was properly in place. The scenes were often idealized from mythology or the ancients: *The Rape of the Sabines, Prometheus Bound.* Landscapes and still lifes were beautiful, proportioned, realistic. Portraits, depicting members of the nobility, were painted in the grand style of Eakins or Gainsborough. The canvas was drawn and painted with careful artistry, and finished in a polished way. Even the nonpainter senses the *telos* embedded therein. The slightest hint of roughness or incompleteness would have ruled it out of the French Salon, whose exhibits set the standard for acceptable painting.

Enter the Impressionists, lighting up the canvas with color, but in a nonclassic way. They suggested rather than defined. Often their paintings were rough-stroked, details omitted. They relied on distance and the viewer's eye to complete the gestalt. Their scenes were common parks, ballets, boats, servants. Their finished product had a rough-hewn look, with an economy of line.

A good example is in the work of Frans Hals. Sometimes, Hals took endless care with his portraits and ended with a classical production, neat and meticulously done. At other times, he went to a tavern and with bold, rough strokes painted the innkeeper or the shepherd boy. Both styles are worthy of the museum, but significantly, the latter style was the wave of the future. Hals and—two centuries later—the Impressionists are close to preachers of modern brief sermons. Classical painters and classical preachers are also blood relations. They wind up with a flourish. The others just drop it and run.

It is no different in music. Listeners still love Brahms and Beethoven and the romantic sounds of Tchaikovsky. However, a new sound is intruding. This sound has jangling chords and odd syncopations. Jazz and the blues have blended with the symphonic; the saxophone and odd percussion instruments have set up stands in the concert hall. It is not that the new music has no rules, but its rules are not the age-old, acceptable rules of the early-twentieth-century conservatory. The ending of the new-style music is of a piece with the rest of it: sometimes blunt, sometimes soft, but never overstated.

8

TAKE SOUNDINGS

Soundings are practice sessions for all or part of the sermon before it is delivered. Soundings, done not once but many times, will often push the phrases around into a more appealing sequence. Parts of a sentence that need stress will often get rearranged after being heard spoken rather than being seen written. Odd, awkward, hard-to-pronounce phrases can be smoothed out or changed. Colorful, concrete nouns can replace faded, abstract ones that may have gone unnoticed on the printed page. The proper amount of repetitions, so much more necessary in spoken discourse than in written, can be added by the preacher, much as the right pinch of seasoning is added by a cook. Balanced and rhythmical construction, which acts as an easier conveyance of thought to a listener, might force its way to the surface. Some of the very cadence that is in the Biblical text may help transform the sermonic sentence.

It is not by chance that so much of the Bible sounds pleasant to the ear. Much of Biblical literature existed first as oral tradition, or else was written for people who caught more by the ear than from the written page. Even after it was written, the oral quality was built in. For instance, in this remark of Job, the balanced phrases make for easy listening as well as for forceful speaking:

> If I have withheld anything that the poor desired,
> or have caused the eyes of the widow to fail,

or have eaten my morsel alone,
and the fatherless has not eaten of it;

. . . .

if I have seen any one perish for lack of clothing,
or a poor man without covering;
if his loins have not blessed me,
and if he was not warmed with the fleece of my sheep;
if I have raised my hand against the fatherless,
because I saw help in the gate,
then let my shoulder blade fall from my shoulder,
and let my arm be broken from its socket. (Job 31:16–22)

Job's sentence is long, but it is put in such a way that it can be listened to easily. The images are concrete, the structure of the sentence has balance, the ideas move swiftly from a series of "if's" to the concluding "then." That sentence was written by someone who had an ear for sound.

Sermons are usually written before they are delivered. This is essential to keep thought within time bounds and to ensure the orderly progression of ideas. However, there is a subtle danger involved in all written manuscripts which are then taken into the pulpit for delivery. What is carried in hand, words on paper that have been written for the eye, are quite different from words on paper that have been written for the ear. Most ministers have had good written English drilled into them from first grade through seminary. The nuts and bolts of spelling and grammar and style were mastered and put into term papers and English compositions. On the other hand, the vocal arts of rhetoric or forensics or even storytelling touched us only slightly. Furthermore, the companions of the academic life, books by the shelfful, assuming they were good books and well written, only reinforced the art of written English, rather than the different skills of spoken English. Even poetry, which nearly always is written for the ear, is nearly always studied by the eye, once it becomes the subject of freshman English. The cadence, the harmonious word combinations, the overall tones of gentleness or abrasiveness that go with certain stanzas, are lost and the poem is blanched, devoid of color. Sermons, like poems, belong to the spoken arts. They must be spoken before the nuances appear. Henry Grady Davis, in his excellent book on homiletics *Design for Preaching,* has a chapter entitled "Writing for the Ear." In it the author suggests:

> When [ministers are] wording their themes or messages, when they are composing their structural assertions, when they are writing their sketch or the sentences or paragraphs of the sermon, when they set down any words whatever, [they] must hear how they sound when spoken, each combination of syllables, each phrase when joined with other phrases to make a sentence, each sentence when joined to others to create the movement of language. Their experience and training as students will not have prepared them for this kind of writing; may even have made it harder. But there is no help for it. They must lay on themselves the discipline of listening to their language as they write until it becomes second nature. Like the deaf Beethoven, they must write a music of language heard by their inner ear.[23]

The insight of the author is keen. We must write for the ear. The problem, however, is that there are few Beethovens who can hear what they write while in the process of writing. Most need to do soundings so that the ear is engaged critically—and in advance of the day the sermon is actually delivered.

The differences between oral and written style were noted long ago. As early as the fourth century B.C., Aristotle said: "It should be observed that each kind of rhetoric has its own appropriate style. The style of written prose is not that of spoken oratory. . . . Both written and spoken have to be known." More specifically, what are the differences? Furthermore, what do the differences have to do with brevity? Much research has been done on the first question in recent years. Gladys L. Borchers, professor of speech at the University of Wisconsin, compiled a list of eighteen rules or suggestions for oral language. Among them are the following observations concerning oral style:

—Sentences are less involved in structure.
—Fragmentary sentences may be used.
—Slang is acceptable.
—Contractions are used more often.

—A greater amount of repetition is not only acceptable but necessary.

—Oral style is more euphonious.

—Concrete words should be used more often.

—The rhythm is different from the rhythm of written style.

If these observations are true, an excellent sermon delivered from the pulpit might make the preacher blush to see it in print. The grammar and sentence structure, the contractions, the personal pronouns, the slang, violate all the rules of freshman English. Indeed, the sermon in perfect English often falls below the interest level, while the spoken style strikes home. Oral style sometimes has a plus, though it may violate "good English." It is the same plus that Pavlova noted in dancing. "If I could have said it," she once observed, "I would not have needed to dance it." Similarly a preacher might say, "If I could have written it, there would have been no need to speak it." Oddly enough, though the differences between the spoken and the written are well known, preachers usually form their sermons using the canons of "good English," forgetting entirely the rules for oral English.

The distinction between the oral and the written has consequences for brevity, especially for psychological brevity. Psychological brevity occurs when a spoken piece seems short, even though it may not be so in duration. The marks of psychological brevity appear when the members of the congregation do not look at their watches or gaze out the window. If the preacher is not afraid to be colorful, and to use crisp, bright language, the sermon will seem shorter. On the other hand, another sermon can be couched in good English, grammatically speaking, and be dull and forbidding. The difference will be as sharp as between a gaily wrapped gift and one wrapped in brown paper, held tight with sealing tape.

Let us consider two approaches to the story of Nicodemus. The first is adequate, but lacking in color.

Adequate: "There is a story in the Gospel of John about a highly-placed man coming to Jesus by night. He was a member of the Sanhedrin, the ruling body of the Jews, and a teacher besides. The story makes two interesting comments about Nicodemus which lead us into the heart of the story. He is obviously an older man, for he asks the question, 'How can a man be born when he is old?' And he is probably a frightened man, for he comes to see Jesus by night when no one is around to observe.

"Many like Nicodemus have problems with faith in middle age. By their experience and position they are expected to have things all worked out; yet, underneath the mask of respectability, they know this is not so, and they long for more. That must have been Nicodemus' frame of mind as he went to see Jesus and got caught up in a discussion of what it means to be born again."

This is not a bad opening, but let us try another which is written more to be sounded than read.

Better: "Picking his way through the dark streets, Nicodemus found the door. He peered this way and that. Did enemy eyes detect him, or puzzled comrades with arched eyebrows? Were there any to speculate about his strange passage?

"To doubt in middle age is scary. To entertain the possibility of new belief cracks the structure of things. Not for children, or even for private citizens, but for prominent figures. Leaders are supposed to have it all worked out. They defend the system, together with their peers. If the establishment doesn't hold firm, chaos comes.

"What a hell to be in! To have to lead when you're lost. To stand for law 'n' order and orthodoxy, while your own beliefs crack and crumble. If we could be destroyed in private, that is bearable. When everything falls apart in full view, that's hell.

"Fortunately, the town slept. The streets held no observers. The wind blew past the shuttered forms of houses.

" 'Pssst! Master! It's Nicodemus,' whispered the Pharisee as he tapped the door. 'Open quickly.'

"The door opened just a crack, then fully. A shaft of light lit the dark. Jesus beckoned the guest inside. Nicodemus had arrived. Safely. In a deeper way than he first surmised."

The styles of these two treatments differ, but there is more than that. The second version has some of the marks that Borchers has found applicable to oral style—more concreteness in verb and noun; a different rhythm; some fragmentary sentences and contractions. Even a touch of profanity. It has a brightness to it that makes the truth it wants to convey, which is the same truth as in the first approach, slightly more appealing.

But, what does sounding have to do with brevity? Let us move to that question. First of all, sounding trains the ear to detect the slightest hint of overtalk, once the preacher knows that verbosity can be a problem. Extemporaneous speakers often get carried away with their subject, or caught in a cul-de-sac which leaves them frantically hunting for the verbal road out. Manuscript readers often do the same, though in a more polished and pedantic way. Good writing, of course, should always avoid verbosity, but in speech the necessity of condensation is more nearly absolute.[24] However, it often takes several soundings before words crunch down compactly. The chief quality of personal communication is that it says a great deal, suggests more, and in very few words. But this takes repeated listening to your own expressions before the congregants assemble.

For instance, here is a short phrase of Dylan Thomas that does the work of many words. He speaks of "a grief ago." It would be interesting to know how many times he had to reshuffle his words before they came into focus in this way. However, "a grief ago" is such an apt expression for his thought, that he uses it as the title of that particular poem. The expression takes the place of many words that might be used for a paraphrase. For instance, we would have said, "at some time in the past, a time filled with feelings of grief."[25] But that paraphrase contains thirteen words, while the original has only three. Furthermore, the three are far better. Such an artful phrase would probably not work in a sermon. It would be obvious as belonging to poetic discourse. Yet there are many ways that come out in soundings where an unusual turn of phrase can do the work of entire sentences, and where sentences can be cut in half. Here are a few examples from *Design for Preaching:*[26]

"We form our opinions and judgments upon the basis of what we have known." (Fourteen words.) "We think as we have known." (Six words.)

"These judgments and opinions then become the basis of our assertions and our activities." (Fourteen words.) "We speak and act as we think." (Seven words).

"We who are within the ranks of those who are standing by the missionary enterprise, must make good our claim that our religion possesses something which cannot be supplied by other religions." (Thirty-two words.) "We who support missions must show that our faith gives what no other can." (Fourteen words, showing the difference between verbosity and forcefulness.)

The first benefit of soundings, then, is to reduce verbiage. Another benefit is the perfection of body language, which can eliminate whole sentences of spoken language. For instance, the simple word "oh" can mean many things depending on the glance of the eye, the position of the hands and shoulders, or the twist of the head. It can mean: "You surprise me"; or "I made a mistake"; or "You're a pain in the neck"; or "You make me so happy"; or "I'm bored"; or "I understand"; or "I don't understand." Probably, if the "Oh" is sounded and acted rightly, the fuller explanation can be omitted.

Body language, even if it shortens a sermon, seems fake to many if it has to be rehearsed. The apparent falseness conjures up the satire in a *Spectator* paper in which Sir Roger de Coverley figures. Addison and Steele picture the baronet leaving his country church after the bishop has preached an eloquent sermon, full of gestures. As he leaves, Sir Roger sees the vestry door open a crack, and sees through the door into the vestry. There, before the mirror, the bishop stands with a self-satisfied smile, making the same gestures with which he closed the sermon. Just so, to practice gestures seems put-on, pompous, prideful. Yet, why should it? The prophets used dramatic skills and were sincere. They broke pitchers, walked in sackcloth, bound themselves, danced. When Jeremiah went down to the potter's shop and broke a pitcher before the eyes of the elders (Jeremiah 19), he didn't have to go into lengthy explanations. Nor did Ezekiel have to speak long on the possibility of a siege at Jerusalem when he lay on the street, bound and surrounded by minimum rations (Ezekiel 4). The prophets did these things, and the body expressed volumes more than their words. Body language, properly "spoken," does this. But, for most of us, practice is needed to make effective use of it; that, and a willingness to admit we have something in common with the drama guild.

A third advantage of practice is pacing, the quickness or slow movement of words. Brevity suggests to some a rapid-fire, machine gun rattle of sentence after sentence. Cram in everything possible. Oh? That's nonsense. Can you read the sign on the truck you passed at 55 miles per hour going the opposite direction? Speed interferes with the reception of meaning unless the delivery is broken by breathers. Yet the need for breathers is sometimes only known after vocalizing the sermon.

There are many ways to control speed, though practice and intuition are required to detect the need for it. Just to pause after a rapid flow of sentences permits assimilation time. In the paragraph above, the language moves fast until the "Oh?" That word, or some substitute, is needed as a brake before the speed picks up again. The same effect can be gotten by humor.

Humor is dangerous. It must be used with care and kept under strict control. Yet, it is valuable. A breath of humor can momentarily relieve concentration and prepare for further concentration. If it is true that the attention span of the average adult is six minutes, a slight smile produced by a slight bit of nonsense permits another six minutes, no questions asked. For instance, an opening development of the text "I bid every one among you not to think of himself more highly than he ought to think" might describe the many ways we overvalue our efforts. If this is followed by the *New Yorker* cartoon (mentioned earlier), or by Robert Burns's "Oh wad some power the giftie gie us . . . ," or by the description of Sir Roger at church, a dash of humor is added without derailing the sermon.

The masterful use of humor is to make it advance thought rather than interrupt it. When you interrupt thought to tell a joke, you have wasted time. The waste may be calculated and needed, but the average brief sermon does not allow for too many such interruptions. It is much better to weave the humor into the fabric of the sermon.

Consider again Edmund Steimle's "Address Not Known." The sermon stresses the amazing thought that in the Bible, contrary to popular opinion, God is more often absent than vividly present to the awareness of his followers. Steimle continues this idea by saying that we often look for God in the wrong places. At this point, the preacher lets us up for a breather. He quotes the story of a Munich comedian, Karl Valentin:

> ... The curtain goes up and reveals darkness; and in this darkness is a solitary circle of light thrown by a street lamp. Valentin, with his long-drawn and deeply worried face, walks around and around this circle of light, desperately looking for something. "What have you lost?" a policeman asks who has entered the scene. "The key to my house." Upon which the policeman joins him in his search; and they find nothing; and after a while, he inquires, "Are you sure you lost it here?" "No," says Valentin, and pointing to a dark corner of the stage: "Over there." "Then why on earth are you looking for it here?" "There is no light over there," says Valentin.[27]

The breather has been inserted deftly, and is an integral part of the sermon. No time is wasted while we chuckle.

Pacing is more than slowing down, and more than inserted humor. The entire sermon has a rhythmic flow. The shorter it is, the more time must be given to the fast/slow rubato. One trick to this end is to write the manuscript in the style of Peter Marshall. It looks like blank verse. It reads with the cadence of poetry. The method commends itself to all who use manuscripts and who wrestle with the intangible factors of pacing. However, even this style of manuscript should *follow* the verbal practice. Other notes, or an outline, can be used for the practice session.

One final benefit of a sermon rehearsal is the possibility of preaching without notes. This is only indirectly related to brevity. The fast/slow rubato mentioned above can be planned and built into the manuscript, though it happens more freely when inspired by the listeners' eyes and the face of the clock. Like the teacher who feels it necessary to "cover" the material, a preacher with a manuscript must stick to it. Other teachers who know the main point of their lesson, and the steps to it, have more freedom to speed up or delete. They usually end up as better communicators.

The preacher should not make a fetish of the skill of preaching without notes. Yet this practice removes the manuscript as a barrier. When a comedian permits his eye to move too obviously to the teleprompter, he allows a mechanical device to block the personal touch. A Saturday "rehearsal" embeds connected sections of the sermon in the mind for instant recall. The development pattern of the sermon is set. The nuance of the story is fresh. Most of all, the emotional tone is added. Practice is to the preacher what the Stanislavsky method is to the actor. You come to the pulpit already "into" your message. An emotional warmth is conveyed with the content. Something of the passion of verbal preparation carries over. It is the passion of preachers who struggle with and discipline their efforts, and who will not settle for the almost-right word, or the half-decent rhythm, or the somewhat-clear sequence of ideas. Instead, they want the just-right word, the smooth flow and pace, and the crisp sequence of thought. Then, perhaps, the heat of the preparation kindles enthusiasm and conviction in those who hear.

The suggestion to practice verbally is not new. In fact, some of the greats used just such a technique. George Buttrick paced his study on Sunday morning mumbling parts of his sermon before the service. He, in turn, tells of arriving early at a garden party in England many years ago. As he walked along beside the high hedges of the formal garden, he heard a voice whispering on the other side of the hedge in deep, guttural tones. It turned out to be Winston Churchill, the speaker of the day, rehearsing what he was going to say. To go over a sermon verbally beforehand is nothing to be ashamed of. When you do this, you are in good company.

9

FEEL COMFORTABLE
WITH SILENCE

One hard-to-get-at aspect of preaching is "the significance of silence." Silence is never neutral. It is not the dead air space which is the dread of radio announcers. It is colored by what is said before it and by what is anticipated afterward, and also by what is going on in the listeners' minds. This must be understood by preachers or they will never learn the art of pausing or the wisdom of sitting down sometime before the usual thirty minutes have passed.

We are afraid of silence. We don't know what to do with it, so we usually try to fill it with something less creative. Robert Raines opens his helpful book *Creative Brooding* with a comment on how hard it is to find the quiet for meditation. He observes how the Muzak loudspeakers make sound omnipresent —in elevators, down corridors, surrounding dentist chairs. And, what Muzak has not covered, the transistorized radio has —on beaches, at picnics, on hikes through the woods, in canoes on the lake. It is almost as if we are afraid to be alone with ourselves, as if the Alone might catch up with our loneliness. T. S. Eliot caught the mechanical reaching for sound in the story of the lady who has just dismissed her lover after another act of meaningless sex. As he departs, she paces the room alone. Then, "She smoothes her hair with automatic hand, and puts a record on the gramophone."[28] Everywhere, the modern mood is to fill the silence with sound, and then we can be comfortable. Against this, we must put in a good word for silence, and learn to take our silence straight, and allow space for some uninterrupted transactions to take place in the mind.

Think for a moment of the variety there is in silence. Silence is never monolithic. It takes definite shape and for specific ends. There is the silence after you hear a sound in the attic. What is it? Did I really hear it? Will it happen again? Is it a good sound or a bad? This silence is one of anxiety that waits further definition. Then, there is the silence of one shoe falling. When will the other one fall? There is no peace of mind until it does. This is the silence of anticipation. Let the other shoe fall. The sooner, the better, since it is almost inevitable. Then, there is the momentary silence between the raising of a conductor's baton and the downbeat. This is the tense moment of readiness, in which all available energy is assembled before the event opens. Some of this feeling is engendered in Revelation, where the apocalyptist says that there was silence in heaven for about half an hour (Rev. 8:1). The divine baton is in the air, and all the players in the drama are waiting for the signal. Or, there is the silence after a question. The expert teacher, having raised a question, doesn't rush in with the answer. She might even end the class on that note, allowing the question to keep prodding until the next day. Silence after the question makes the question effective. There is the silence of bidding prayer. The heading is given in some specific manner, but so is the silence, so that the listener can take the thought along some personal paths. Silence is not just plain home-grown silence. It comes in various forms, and has a useful part to play if preachers recognize this and can capitalize on it. Part of the economy of language is to recognize the eloquence of silence. Many ideas can go without saying.

Silence is the ally of the preacher, especially helpful in the art of pacing. Pacing relies on "blips" of silence. Sentences, paragraphs, running phrases are separated by pauses long enough for listeners to catch their breath and put it together. The spoken words themselves have a pace—a varied rhythm. The pace cannot be as regular as the clicking of a train on railroad tracks, or the congregation will fall asleep. Nor is it quite as regular as the stanzas of a hymn, lest it convey a feeling to the audience that the sermon is too artful, too contrived. The pace is more like that of a race horse in the hands of a jockey like Steve Cauthen. There is a plan of where you want to be at what point around the track, when to hold back and when to spurt, and when to hit the home stretch with all that's left. That is the art of pacing the words. But, in between groups of words are the blips of silence which are part of the effectiveness of all well-spoken addresses. The more experienced the speaker, the more silence can be played to perfection.

Consider public speakers as diverse as stand-up comedians, lyric poets, and preachers. Take the best in each field and listen for the times they wait for the words to take effect. Oswald Hoffmann, for many years preacher on *The Lutheran Hour,* opened an address at Princeton with humor worthy of a comedian. It involved Swedes and Norwegians, and the jovial rivalry between these ethnic groups in the Midwest. A Swede and a Norwegian meet in Minnesota. Ollie Olsen is coming from the lake with fish pail and pole. The Swede asks, "Where you bin, Ollie?" "Vot you tink I bin? Fishin'!" "Tell you vot, Ollie. If I guess how many fish you got in dat pail, how 'bout givin' me von of dem?" "You guess how many fish in dat pail, and I give you both of dem!" (pause) The Swede thinks, and guesses. "Five!" (pause) Ollie thinks. "Sorry. You missed it by two." (pause)

The pauses are for laughter. They also are for wide-eye mugging, humping shoulders, throwing up hands on the part of the raconteur. And the pause can be expanded by a virtuoso, because it only clears the air of one laugh so that the next laugh can be more of a guffaw.

By contrast, listen to a good reader of Tennyson's "Break, Break, Break." The words are printed, but they need a cue sheet for reading. Some of the lines are:

> Break,—break,—break,—
> On thy cold gray stones, O Sea!
> And I would that my tongue could utter
> The thoughts that arise in me.

The repetition of "Break, break, break" evokes the waves that hit rocks and recede back to the sea. It conveys the way the poet has been hit by grief after the death of a child. But waves don't break in waltz time. They hit, and re-collect force before they hit again. The longer the time to swirl back, the more forceful the next wave.

Many otherwise effective talks are spoiled because the timing is poor, and the listener listens off balance and can't quite keep up. The signal is given that the speaker is nervous, or that the material is not under control, or that much speaking will score more points. In any case, the thinking the listeners must do between the words is not possible. The quiet time is choked out during which the fuller reception was meant to take place.

The other danger is that the silences will be too long. They are blops of silence rather than blips. Blops of silence are invitations to a congregation to make grocery lists, or work on the research project, or just pay a visit to Xanadu. The preacher should know the darting power of the mind, and the visual power of the eye, all the while he or she takes advantage of silence. Average readers cover six hundred words per minute, but even fast speakers can push out only a quarter of that amount. Therefore, pauses must put limits on, or give channels to, the minds of the listeners. Otherwise they won't use the silence creatively, to reflect on the theme that the preacher proposes. However, once aware of that danger, and willing to risk the Scylla and Charybdis of racing or dawdling, skilled preachers use the constant interplay of words and silence. They can make ten words do the work of hundreds. They can take whatever time they usually use for the sermon, and speak less while "saying" more. They might even, by making the sermon a shared event, trim the sail of the sermon in the interest of greater force and movement.

One great and eloquent silence in Scripture demonstrates the place of silence in relation to driving the message home. Elijah, the despondent prophet, ran away into the desert, and God was in pursuit. The prophet holed up in a cave, and God closed in with a message. The usual sequence is: "The LORD passed by, and a great and strong wind rent the mountains, and broke in pieces the rocks before the LORD, but the LORD was not in the wind; and after the wind an earthquake, but the LORD was not in the earthquake; and after the earthquake a fire, but the LORD was not in the fire; and after the fire a still small voice. . . . And behold, there came a voice to him, and said, 'What are you doing here, Elijah?' " (I Kings 19:11–13). On first reading it looks as if there was a lot of natural fanfare, and then God whispered his message. It is more probable that "still small voice" is translatable as "an absolute stillness." It was a silence full of anticipation, prefaced by a display of God's majesty, and followed by the chance for Elijah to stand in awe and be ready to listen. When the desert stage was set, God slipped in his words in a whisper—terse and to the point—and rested his case. Elijah caught the words—after the silence had made him ready.

10

LET THE LISTENER
DO THE TRAVELING

If preachers assume they must trace out all the ramifications of a subject, they will not only be long-winded; they will also forget the possibilities in listeners to travel for miles on their own. Think about the listener. The sermon's length takes place in that person, not in the manuscript. Strike the right chord, and the overtones will play at the receiving end in all combinations. The listener will carry the thought farther and in more directions than the speaker ever imagined. This can easily be checked by listening to the many after-service comments. The preacher wonders where all those interpretations and suggestions came from.

It is often assumed that the sermon must be complex and that the listener is simply a blank page to be imprinted. The reverse is true. The listener's mind is complex, filled with a million messages, quite capable of taking new material and putting it in untold combinations. Consider an analogy from the railroads. Most sermons start out of the terminal on a single track, and then select various switches and trunk lines until they arrive at the destination on another single track. The route, the criss-cross of track, and the switches are in the preacher's control. The preacher expects the passengers to be on the train when it arrives at the destination so that they can all get off together. Fortunately or unfortunately, the passengers do not all stay with the train. They get off en route and travel to other cities. This is not all bad. It saves preachers from traveling to every spot the listeners want to visit, an impossible task. Better for preachers to reach their destination by the most direct route, but to realize that their passengers are traveling to all parts of the country. If you are the preacher, be glad you were able to start them on trips they might not otherwise have taken.

This point was brought home to me while reading a poem by John Holmes called "The New View." I realized how different the reader's reception can be from the meaning the author had in mind. Here is the poem:

> There was an old stump of an old tree standing
> All naked of bark, and brown, and ten feet tall
> In the wrong place for our summer pleasure.
> I pushed it over. I was glad to see it fall.
>
> Let it lie there in the high grass till rotted.
> The roots broke when I rocked it where it stood,
> The trunk split, and the shell in half round pieces
> Opened, and let fall something that had been wood.
>
> But there were bees in it. Bees have a business
> Not safely suddenly outraged by anything.
> Nothing is left to an old man but his anger
> And I had hurried death that needs no hurrying.
>
> The stump was gone, we could look further and greener.
> It was two June days before my wound was well.
> That was all we got, and we had the spoiled honey
> For sorrow, and a new view past where the tree fell.

(From John Holmes, *Writing Poetry,* published by The Writer, Inc. Copyright © 1960 by John Holmes.)

I thought I had the meaning of the poem in hand. Any preacher who has tangled with an old, outworn institution knows the feeling. The Ladies' Aid, or was it the Retired Men's Club, or perhaps the Prayer Meeting, really did need to be chopped down. So it came to pass that the preacher spoke to the few straggling members, suggesting that the group should disband and put its money into the general treasury. Little did the preacher know that he'd feel the wrath of the bees in that stump, their ability to sting. He got over the welts. The view was better, but there was also a certain nostalgia, a sorrow of spoiled honey.

Where did my interpretation come from? My experience in church work. I am sure that if I checked with the housewife, the truck driver, the schoolteacher, the politician, I would find that they took the poem down another track entirely. As it happens, the author, John Holmes, had his own background for the poem. He really did live in a summer home that had a tree blocking the view. The tree was pushed over, and the author really was stung. However, superimposed on this happening was an argument he had with his father, who was as venerable as the tree. The father gave the son a stinging rebuke. Without this experience, the poem would not have happened. Yet the detail of the author's feelings would hardly be discoverable by some other reader unless the author shared them.

Relating this again to the sermon, the meaning is clear. The preacher's mind-set, which produces a sermon, is vastly different from anyone else's in the congregation. The preacher cannot know everyone's train of thought, nor is that necessary. The congregant will do his or her own traveling for miles and for hours past the sermon time. The extension of the sermon is in the listener's mind rather than in the preacher's manuscript. Therefore, let the listener do the traveling.

PART III
DOES
BREVITY
COMPROMISE?

I have argued that brevity is a function of effective communication. Be briefer in the pulpit—because the twentieth-century congregation expects brevity, theology sanctions it, and effective proclamation of the gospel utilizes it. To this end, ten guidelines were suggested to assist preachers toward a briefer style. However, an insidious question hovers over the argument and the program. Has anything been compromised in the process? In particular, has the message been offered to the goddess Popularity, and have the messengers sold their souls for a mess of pottage?

The same brevity that leads to effective communication can also be popular with the masses. Since it is very hard to untangle what is effective from what is successful, the thesis of this book can be criticized as a crash program for statistical success rather than as a means to better preaching. If that is so, beware! Anything that attracts great numbers is understandably suspect. The gospel is never popular with the masses once it is really heard. Biblical prophets and apostles often ended their ministry in some form of martyrdom. They lost the crowds, and were lone voices in the wilderness of their times. We have had enough martyrs like Martin Luther King in the last two decades to remind preachers that the cross always hovers around any faithful communication of the gospel, whether short or long. Therefore, if indeed brevity does attract more persons, the numerical success may be a judgment far more than a commendation. Can any message be popular without a bow and a scrape toward mammon?

Before pursuing this argument, let us question the premise. It is not really axiomatic that brevity will bring crowds or be popular. Perhaps this style will, and perhaps it won't. Furthermore, it would be hard to distinguish what was the drawing factor in a terse popular sermon. Was it the brevity or the content that made it popular? The same question could be asked about the unpopular but brief sermon. Was it the message or the person who delivered it that made it unpopular? We have already referred to Lincoln's Gettysburg Address as an example of brief, appropriate oratory. Press coverage after the event was not conclusive that great words had been spoken. The *New York Tribune* and many other newspapers reported that there was applause at five places in the address, but responsible witnesses also record that it was formal and perfunctory. The *Chicago Tribune* did say: "The dedicatory remarks of President Lincoln will live among the annals of man." On the other hand, the *Chicago Times* alleged that "Mr. Lincoln did most foully traduce the motives of the men who were slain at Gettysburg in his reference to 'a new birth of freedom.' Not a new freedom, but the old is what they died for." Then the *Times* continued, "The cheek of every American must tingle with shame as he reads the silly, flat and dish-watery utterances of the man who has to be pointed out to intelligent foreigners as the President of the United States."[29] What does this type of reporting tell us about Lincoln's message? Was it great oratory, or great oratory misconstrued? Was it popular? If the test of time is needed to prove its greatness, does the word "popular" apply? What is popular has an immediate appeal. It is what goes over at the time. Its force spreads quickly and it is quoted with esteem. Again, was Lincoln's address popular?

The answer to these questions is ambiguous. For some, after Gettysburg, the message and the style immediately clicked. What Lincoln said spoke to their condition. Even Edward Everett, the main orator of the day, recognized this. The next day, he sent a note to Lincoln which was more than a courtesy. "I should be glad if I could flatter myself that I came as near to the central idea of the occasion in two hours as you did in two minutes." So, too, the *Springfield Republican,* which veered from its first opinion that "Lincoln was honest, but a Simple Susan." Its comment referred to the speech as "a perfect gem; deep in feeling, compact in thought and expression, and tasteful and elegant in every word and comma, [having the merit of] unexpectedness in its verbal perfection and beauty." Thus, some reacted immediately and with enthusiasm to what was spoken. Meanwhile the crowds and the majority of papers reporting the event held at best a lukewarm if not antagonistic reaction. There is no reason to assume that the compact statement of the gospel will fare any better. We cannot say in advance that it will be applauded any more than the long form, even though the preacher hopes that brevity in the service of the gospel will gain more hearers and capture more of their allegiance.

Perhaps this latter desire needs to be examined. Is it right to want to be popular? To feel the compulsion to appeal more broadly? To have busy, pressured people stop and listen? Granted that masses exist outside the church, should this in itself drive preachers to attempt to reverse the trend through a different style of preaching or through a different anything else? As Robert Evans of Hartford Seminary noted, "What God demands of his church is not growth but faithfulness, a faithfulness that carries no promise of growth, healthfulness or anything else, since the Holy Spirit alone can give these."[30] The advice to preachers that follows from this line of thought seems clear. Be faithful to the message, forget style, and let God be God. The advice in its practical import is not far removed from that given by old-fashioned predestinarians, who rested in the good feeling that people respond when God wills that they do, and not before. It is one thing to note that great numbers stay away from church and quite another to take any undue initiative to try to attract them.

A classic form of this objection was the response of a Calvinist minister to William Carey. Carey was one of the fathers of the modern missionary movement in England in the late eighteenth and early nineteenth centuries. When he started to present his ideas of missions, the Calvinist replied, "Young man, when God wants to save the heathen, He'll do it without any help from you or me." Just so, the modern Calvinist can continue to preach traditional fare in traditional ways and make the question of effectiveness part of the doctrine of predestination. Thus, God will use our sermons or not use them depending on his own good pleasure. From this point of view, there is no need for mass appeal through brevity.

However, the central focus of our subject has not been mass appeal through brevity. The primary point is effective communication—based on faithfulness to the gospel, which is the bedrock of effective Christian communication. In a secondary way, brevity may be appealing, and probably will attract more. That remains to be seen. The effectiveness of brevity might even be tested statistically, providing more preachers attend to this aspect of their preaching. However, assuming that wider appeal does take place, is that all bad? It is no particular mark of faithfulness to the gospel that its appeal should decline, or that the attempt to make its communication appealing should be ruled out as unworthy. Certainly there are some cues in the incarnation that indicate the mind of God in this regard. A God who takes the initiative in the incarnation would expect preachers also to take the initiative by placing the Word in the kind of flesh that common people will respond to. The Biblical apostles and prophets, even those who were ultimately rejected, were a breed who would reach for any allusion, any thought form, any argument to get the message through to as many as possible. When Paul says, "I appeal to you . . . by the mercies of God . . ." (Rom. 12:1); or again, "My heart's desire . . . for [Israel] is that they may be saved" (Rom. 10:1), you catch the note of wide-ranging passion. He speaks (to use old-fashioned rhetoric) as a dying man to dying men. While mass appeal through brevity is not the main point, neither is it one that needs an apology. There might even be room for some of the gutsy approach of the founder of the Salvation Army, William Booth. As he was embarking for a visit to America, with bands playing on the dock, someone criticized the public display as unseemly for a Christian movement. To this person Booth replied, "If I thought I could win one more to Christ by doing a handstand and beating a tambourine with my feet, I would do it." That, laudable not for technique but for motive, is a refreshing, aggressive approach.

Of course, the desire to appeal to the masses can be perverted. There is a long tradition of wanting to attract numbers for the wrong reasons. While Moses was on the mountain receiving the commandments, Aaron had reached the crowds in the desert below with a golden calf. His word was short and appealing: "These are your gods, O Israel" (Ex. 32:4). And the people danced their approval. Or switch the scene to Samaria, where the two kings, Jehoshaphat and Ahab, were trying to decide whether to wage war on Ramoth-gilead or negotiate peace (I Kings 22). The court prophets were sought, and they quickly sensed the message that was wanted. "Go up [and do battle], for the LORD will give it into the hands of the king." One of the prophets, to demonstrate the word and drive it home, grabbed two animal horns. This is the way you'll push the enemy back, he said, as he made ramming motions, holding the horns to his head. A very popular message, but self-serving and deceptive. The kings went, and the battle was lost.

Switch scenes to the days of Jeremiah. His message seemed prickly, distasteful, unpatriotic—and long. Jehoiakim the king received a written copy of it, and pared it down with his knife like an apple. Each strip was thrown into the fire (Jeremiah 36). On the other hand, Jeremiah's antagonists, another generation of court prophets, had a simple and short message. Jeremiah records that they kept ringing the changes on peace: "They have healed the wound of my people lightly, saying 'Peace, peace,' when there is no peace." (Jer. 6:14). This tradition, of attractive, popular, but erroneous preaching goes back through the centuries, and always raises the red flag above any suggestion that ministers have a responsibility to be popular. In fact, some take mass appeal as the proof that the gospel has been sold for thirty pieces of silver, as if an idol of the goddess Popularity has been erected as a substitute for the cross.

We must admit that court prophets exist in every generation —in *some* large churches, *some* mass meetings, *some* popular radio and television shows. To separate true from false prophets has never been easy, particularly when you are contemporary with the proclamation. The Bible can be the champion of many causes, only a few of which are policies of the kingdom. Furthermore, some of the most bizarre theories and promises attract so many adherents that it is no wonder mass appeal has been identified in the minds of many as the sign of unfaithfulness.

However, there is a world of difference between popularity as an idol and popular preaching. Only the former perverts the gospel, though both can draw huge followings. To set up popularity as an idol means that the preacher wants to be in the spotlight, ready for applause and fame. He or she becomes a celebrity who has happened on a flashy presentation. In this frame of mind, the preacher would look to brevity or to anything else as the quick road to that goal, and not worry about truth or the cutting edge of the message or the fact that sometimes the prophets were stoned, sawn asunder, or put into prison. The idol of popularity so fascinated Simon of Samaria that he offered Peter money in exchange for gospel power, little caring about the real purpose of the gift or the obedience the gift presumed (Acts 8:18ff.). "Simony" became the term for buying or selling a church office. But wanting the preaching gift for the wrong reasons could well go by the name of "simony." On the other hand, the preacher who wants to do true popular preaching is only concerned with the desire to be heard by as many as possible, without wanting to be in the limelight. Such preaching is in the mold of Jesus' public utterances, which contained common metaphor and deep conviction so that the common people heard him gladly. The idolization of preaching and popular preaching are poles apart, even though both involve numbers of listeners.

Perhaps we should stop using the numbers game either to prove or disprove faithfulness to the Christian message or the effectiveness of a sermon's thrust. Too many times adherents justify their movement or message by the numbers who attend meetings or make contributions. An old advertisement for bananas used to argue, "Two million monkeys can't be wrong," but this hardly proves the value of bananas. Just as often those who attack movements and messages do so by putting reverse English on the ball. They argue that because a meeting or a message has attracted thousands, it must inevitably be subchristian. Many prophets of the '60s, for instance, didn't feel good about themselves or their churches until they started to lose followers. The truth is that good preaching sometimes attracts and sometimes repels, and numbers really prove nothing. However, let no one think mass appeal need be a mark of unfaithfulness. Sometimes Jesus had so many followers that his enemies were aghast. "The world has gone after him" (John 12:19). At other times, he stood alone. "All the disciples forsook him and fled" (Matt. 26:56). It did not mean that suddenly he had become a poor communicator, or that his message had lost its power.

Recently, Martin Marty responded to one of the directors of the Schuller Institute, Wilbert B. Eichelberger. Marty felt the Schuller organization to be saying that if preachers were true to the Word of God they would repeat Schuller's numerical success. Eichelberger thought Marty to have alleged that numerical success was a faint mark of the beast. In clarifying his position, Marty strikes a balanced position on the place of numbers in the Christian movement: "I am always concerned about the morale of the very faithful people in store fronts, village churches, declining rural situations, urban ghettos, or unjust cultures, where to be faithful may mean many things other than growth or success. . . . [On the other hand] it is in my eyes as in yours laziness to deny the Great Commission and then blame one's failures on the claim that there is a greater integrity in decline, as many mainline church folks do. . . ."[31] Numbers, then, neither prove nor disprove faithfulness, and the mere fact that brevity may end up being popular in no way compromises the gospel.

Can the same thing be said of preachers? What will happen to their integrity? If they turn from hefty sermons, will they become light, airy dilettantes? Some might fear that the brevity this book calls for could ultimately compromise the preacher. Some could argue that preachers of briefer sermons will make light of scholarship. Books will be ignored. The new breed will laugh at etymologies of words, historical backgrounds of passages, the input of textual criticism. Scholarly journals will not be subscribed to, or else will lie on the shelf unread. The gulf between the seminary classroom and the pulpit will grow greater until all communication breaks down. This would not suit most preachers, who still hold the ideal of a scholarly pulpit presentation, even if busy parish life prevents the pursuit of it. They see themselves as of the university and seminary, steeped in ancient and modern theology, knowledgeable in Greek if not in Hebrew. Like Melanchthon, they are able to see both sides of every issue. They pride themselves on this, and avoid simplistic answers. They have received the mantle of the prophets and stand in a noble tradition. To suggest that they are responsible for making the Christian message appealing jars their self-image, particularly when they remember the oil paintings that lined the classroom walls, paintings of scholars who never smile, but who possessed great erudition. It seems to many graduates that those pictures would self-destruct if they had to look down on graduates who entertained the idea of preaching briefly, particularly if this meant leaving scholarship behind.

In deference to the scholars, it may be admitted that the short sermon does have its limitations. All the background of Scripture passages cannot be given. Some important points cannot be driven home. Some truths will come through as overstated, since they cannot be balanced with modifying counterstatement. All of this is true. The short sermon is a reminder that every sermon is a heresy. If it stresses the holiness and otherness of God, it may forget the immanence. If the sermon speaks the language of grace, it may omit for that time the language of responsibility. All that the short sermon can do, as over against a longer one, is to present drill samplings in hopes that a ten-inch core is testing the same vein as a twenty-inch core. Yet, considering what the great preachers of yesterday were able to say, the short sermon seems a pale reflection. The limitations are tremendous.

Nevertheless, let no one say that the type of preaching advocated in this book undermines scholarship. To preach so that many will listen is scholarly work too. Good pulpit work that ends in briefer sermons is time-consuming and demanding. It requires endless reading, the extension of intellectual antennae to pick up the vibrations of the times. It demands that attention be given to the findings of the scholarly teachers, if not to their step-by-step procedures. It may overstate a conclusion to make a point. It may spice up a passage to draw attention. But, it wants to communicate God's good news and get the widest possible hearing for that gospel.

This is hard work. To live with the Scriptures and find passages that speak to you, and to ponder how to share these insights without dumping the whole load of insight on the congregation's plate; to roam through the world and be sensitive to playwrights, novelists, scientific journals, and chance bits of conversation, as well as to commentaries; to work for the apt phrase and the easy sequence of ideas instead of lecture-room thoroughness; the word for this is "Whew!"

We have limited the word "scholarship" too much and confined it within classrooms and libraries. Sometimes, the word has become synonymous with "difficult to understand," "erudite," "dull." Scholars may smile knowingly when practical men and women of affairs are given honorary degrees at graduations, as if those honored are simply patrons of the institution, or popular figures, but certainly not scholars. Nonsense. Effectiveness in the popular realm requires a scholarship all its own, and those who succeed in it are perhaps more worthy of accolades than those who never leave their studies. Let me illustrate.

In the 1750's, in Colonial America, there were thoughtful Indian leaders who expressed themselves forcefully in encounters with the white man. These leaders were highly cultured by their society's standards, even though the settlers and administrators would group them together under the general term "savages." One such outstanding Indian was Canasatego, chief of the Onondaga tribes. He received an invitation from the Virginia legislature to send twelve of his braves to the superior schools of Virginia for training. He turned down the offer with the comment, "We tried that in New England, only to receive our warriors back unable to build canoes, track animals or survive in the wilderness." "Suppose," he continued, "you send twelve of your boys to us so that we can train them in what we know of the forest."[32] Canasatego was right. Scholarship comes in many forms. There is a scholarship of the classroom, and a scholarship of the forest.

The medical profession has noted that the general practitioner is in a field of scholarship as much as the specialist in the teaching hospitals. Up to a few years ago, medical students, at a certain point in their preparation, decided either to become specialists or enter old-fashioned general practice. The status of the term "scholar" went with the specialist. The G.P.'s were loved, and dealt with the masses, but they didn't have the savvy that was expected from the specialist. Today, G.P.'s can still be loved, and still deal with the masses, but their field is becoming a specialty called "family practice." The field requires continuing education and periodic exams to maintain the high standards. The doctors who are in family practice still turn to the specialists, but they know some things about applying medicine broadly that the specialists do not know. Just so, ministers who undertake pulpit work seriously are specialists in the field of communication, who need make no apology as if they had left a scholarly pursuit.

Perhaps the real question is not whether briefer preaching, which may end up as popular preaching, will ultimately compromise the preacher or the message. The real question is whether preachers are willing to commit themselves to the hard work this type of scholarship demands. One of the great American biographers, Catherine Drinker Bowen, has described the tiring work of finding a topic and tracking down her material, then deciding to end her research and start to write. But tirelessly she filled a lifetime producing authentic and readable accounts of great lawyers, statesmen, and musicians. Her motto for writing was self-chosen: "Will the reader turn the page?"[33]

Once, she was asked to attend a conference of history teachers. To her surprise and amusement, some of the scholars held her in disdain, as if she belonged to the "lower" field of entertainment. A mere popularizer! One young scholar asked how her books were selling. After she told him, a high number by any standard, he said, "Goodness, I wish I could take a year off and write something that was popular." Little did he know that Bowen took five years to research and write her biography of John Adams, collecting material, visiting Braintree where Adams lived, reading the books of his library, catching the spirit of the colonies. Her writing was not something dashed off once she decided to take a "year off." It was the work of a lifetime. Furthermore, the young man and Catherine Bowen were both scholars, even though he did not realize it. The one aimed at historical truth; the other wanted to make historical truth attractive.

Here, then, are two kinds of scholarship, each right in its place: the scholarship of classroom erudition, and the scholarship of convincing pulpit presentation. Ministers choose the latter as their mandate, because they are interested not merely in searching out the gospel truth but in making that truth attractive. The "how" of preaching is always superimposed on the "What shall I preach?" If these two are ever divorced, then preachers would lose their authenticity as preachers, however authentic they may be in other capacities. Perhaps in other decades and other cultures, brevity may not have figured at all in the "how" of preaching. In fact it may be the mark of dilettantes, what Paul calls "peddlers of the word" (II Cor. 2:17). But our day is different. Our people respond to truth that is compacted before being presented. Therefore, when Paul tells Titus to "adorn the doctrine of God" (Titus 2:10), or when God instructs Habakkuk to wait for the message and then write the vision down plainly, so that he who runs can read (Hab. 2:2), that easily translates into the thesis of this book. Be brief about it.

PART IV
SAMPLES

What do briefer sermons look like? How do they flow? feel? come through? What follows is a sampling of sermons. They come from those special occasions during Lent or at Communion when sermons must enter and leave quickly, often by the side door. They are short, yet sermon length is relative. A longer sermon is still short if it grabs the issue posthaste and pushes it to the center in a briefer way than a host of other words might do. Each of the following sermons can be preached within ten minutes, and each fitted the occasion for which it was crafted. However, the need to be brief at certain times carries over into normal Sunday mornings, so that even these sermons get compacted to the benefit of both sermon and listener. Without a doubt, most Sunday sermons could be shaved by at least a few minutes with no great loss of impact.

In any case, the sermons included here illustrate brevity. They are not illustrations of great sermons, or of remarkable topics. Martin Marty suggests that Protestantism is divided into a two-party system: one the "Private" party which accents individual salvation, and the other the "Public" party which addresses the social order.[34] My background has been shaped more by the former, and the topics have that flavor. Those who wish both excellent sermons and "Public" topics will have to read Harry Emerson Fosdick, Ernest Campbell, and William Sloane Coffin, that trio of prophetic voices from Riverside Church.[35] They are not necessarily specialists in brevity, but it must be added that an amateur dealing with any of their topics would babble on endlessly. A better training in the articulate handling of "Public" topics with maximum word efficiency is found in Rod MacLeish's *The Guilty Bystander,* [36] though these pieces are not sermons. I offer the following sermons without defending them on any other grounds except that they aim at the conciseness mandated by the "guidelines" of Part II.

One thing more, and this concerns the style of presenting these sermons. The page gives a blank verse appearance, akin to the style of Peter Marshall or, more recently, B. Davie Napier.[37] There are two reasons for this. On the one hand, the sermons reflect more accurately the flow of my voice: the places where phrases tumble along, where they meander, and where they pause with an unspoken "Selah" (Stop! Think on this). I do not use a manuscript in the pulpit, and I never write a complete manuscript beforehand, thinking that it gets in the way of naturalness of speech and the freedom I wish to have with the words. However, since a manuscript is often called for, this form helps somewhat to notate the rhythm of the actual sermon without detracting from the content.

On the other hand, this particular form recalls the significant ways in which a sermon has the qualities of a poem. There is always the search for the word with proper connotations, just as in poetry. There must always be attention to words that sound right as well as have the right meaning. This, too, is the mark of a poem. There are also the sentences that parallel and reinforce each other, much as in Hebrew poetry. This is seen much better when a paragraph is reworked into a stanza form.

The danger in comparing a sermon to a poem is that it may throw the sermon into the realm of the aesthetic rather than the prophetic. This, as any reader of Kierkegaard knows, would be anathema. And yet, even a modern poet would not simply wish to hurl a beautiful image devoid of truth and bite. A preacher should understand poet Marianne Moore's desire that words, as used in sermon or poem, should not spoil "the lion's leap."

I AM THE WAY
A Sermon for Would-be Pilgrims
John 14:6

Jesus said, "I am the Way!"

Maybe my old professor was right.
He caught me in a moment of depression,
   confused about my vocation,
     upset with myself that I had lost direction.
"Solvitur ambulando," he said.
"It is solved by walking."

Maybe that's the only way to know the truth of Jesus'
contention,
   to know "He is the Way," not as an academic
   statement,
     but as a truth felt in the viscera.

When a small, select segment of Christians feel they
have arrived,
   and you haven't.
When a much larger segment wonder about either goal
or path,
When we live in a humanity that meanders with a
mazey motion,
   the hard assurance of Jesus is delightfully
   refreshing:
"I am the Way!"

The Way means the road,

the highway, the path
　by which to get there;
As opposed to briers,
　　　woods,
　　　　　marshes,
　　　　　　bogs.
If you have ever stumbled through a thicket, having cut
cross-country, and then found the path or the paved
road,
　you know the importance of the way,
　　the sheer safety of it;

And the romance of it!

Not bumper-to-bumper roads,
But the line of white that cuts through a valley,
　or curves around a mountain,
　　or disappears into the horizon.

The road suggests movement,
　　　　　adventure,
　　　　　　sights,
　　　　　　　things to talk about,
　　　　　　　　progress toward a destination.

Is that why Jesus called himself the Way,
　and tied it so closely to Life?

"I am the Way . . . and the Life."

Let's explore some possibilities:

The Christian faith has never been an arrival.
It's a traveling.
It's not saying, "Whew, I made it."
　"Let's unpack our bags."
　"Journey's end."
It is being on the right road.
Early Christians were followers of the Way.

This is spoken against two kinds of people.

Foremost are the smug.

They have all the answers.
  They never see through a glass darkly.
    They have "arrived," and are not ashamed to say
    so.
New times? New thoughts? Future shock?
There must be something wrong with the times.
There is nothing wrong with us.

Usually this type looks back to some Golden Age.
  There were giants in the land in those days.
    If only we could regain Paradise!
They would never understand Paul, who late in life
confessed,
  "Not that I have already obtained this or am already
  perfect."
Nor would they appreciate the *bon mot* of John
Robinson, pastor to the Pilgrims:
  "The Lord hath more truth and light yet to break
  forth out of His holy word."
Their theme? "Give me that old-time religion. . . .
  It was good for my father,
    And it's good enough for me."

This type, apart from misconceiving the nature of the
Christian faith, are hard on the rest who seem to be
traveling a road, and struggling to make it.

A second group who will not appreciate the Way are
Panacea Christians.
They want instant answers.
Some don't seem to care where the answer comes from
either.
If it is from a minister, fine!
If it is from a famous faith healer, fine!
If it is from the far out, that seems fine, too!
  The occult,
    astrology,

    strange sects,
      tarot cards—
Any source will do if the breakthrough occurs.

To this group, Jesus will be disappointing.
He does not say: Unpack your bags and step this way.
  Your search is over;
    It's the end of the road.
Quite the reverse:
Follow me!
There is the beck and call of the open road,
  and strange sights along the road,
    and the chance to work things out.
"There's no resting place down here."
Come, start to travel. You have not arrived.

    "Only the road, and the dawn, the sun and the
    wind and the rain,
    And the watchfire under the stars, and sleep, and
    the road again."

This theme is played fugue-like in Scripture.
There were heroes of faith who set out, "not knowing
where they were going."
There were exodus tribes who were reminded, "You
have not passed this way before."
There were disciples in the upper room,
  baffled,
    bewildered,
      thrust, against their desire, into a new phase.
To these Jesus says, "I am the Way."

This line of reasoning, however, requires a further
statement of faith:

    God knows the way.

Believe that, and you'll make it.
Hang on to that assurance, and take heart.
Believe it like Daniel Boone in cocky confidence.

"Were you ever lost in the wilderness?" they asked
him.
"Naw," he replied.
"Of course, there was a time when I was slightly
bewildered for four days!"
People like that are the ones who make it
For them, *solvitur ambulando,* "It is solved by
walking."

It is a comfort in strange areas to be going with
someone
who knows the terrain,
  who can point to shortcuts
    or who can argue why the longer road is better,
      who can save you some dead ends.
Jesus Christ is this for the Christian.

He wants to be this for all the baffled.
The original context of the Way was an atmosphere of
confusion.
The disciples were in the upper room.
The cross was hours away.
They felt let down,
    afraid,
      uncertain of the plan.
To these Jesus said, "I am the Way." *Solvitur
ambulando.*

Who has not felt like those disciples at some time?

  Middle-aged men, wondering about job security.
    Will the economy support them?
    Can they keep pace with the young men coming
    along?

  Middle-aged women sensing estrangement in
  marriage.
    What does aging do to love?
    What form does revival take?

Young men and women starting out in life, not
knowing how to earn a living and escape entrapment
in values they seriously question.

Older workers looking at retirement.
   Will they retire into nothingness?
   Can they still find meaning?
   Will their pension support them in the search?

Countless people of all ages express some form of
Philip's desire,
   "Show us the Father, and it sufficeth us."
To all these, Jesus says, "I am the Way."
   Nothing more,
         but nothing less.

There is a way.
It's an unfolding way.
The denouement of it is not mechanical,
   nor clearly marked.
It is shrouded in mystery. And yet . . .
It exists. *Solvitur ambulando.*

One of the great hymns of search is autobiographical.
John Henry Newman, Anglican, soon to become Roman
Catholic,
   writer, theologian,
     preacher of note,
Was confused enough at one point in life to run away.
He traveled south to Italy.
He boarded a boat to circle back to France.
He stood on the bow on a foggy day,
   feeling the blend of attitude and atmosphere.

In his pondering, the lines came to him,
   "Lead kindly light, amid the encircling gloom,
    Lead thou me on . . ."
That hymn is a statement of faith.
It expresses the feeling of those who must walk as

followers of the Way.
It is satisfied if only to confess, "one step enough for
me."

Therefore, I am describing the Christian life as a
pilgrimage,
  not as a destination.
This will bother some.
They like the security of a city,
  not the uncertainty of a road.
But frankly, this is the way of romance and adventure.
Most may even prefer it to "arriving."
Luther, for instance, once remarked that if God had all
the answers in his right hand,
  and the struggle to reach those answers in his left,
    he would choose God's left hand.

Are there any takers for this?

No matter. That's the way it is.
Solvitur ambulando.
"It is solved by walking."
"Follow me," said Jesus.

"I am the Way."

DO YOU WANT TO BE HEALED?

John 5:1–9

Some questions Jesus asked are hard to avoid.
They step out of the mist,
    stand in our way,
        refuse to move to one side or the other,
           demand an answer.
Here's one:

    Do you want to be healed?

The question was directed to a paralytic in Jerusalem.
The man had been paralyzed for thirty-eight years.
He lay in a crowd alongside a pool that had miraculous power.
The Bible says that periodically an angel troubled the waters,
    and whoever stepped in first after this was healed.

This man never made it.
Day after day, and for thirty-eight years, someone always beat him to it.

"Do you want to be healed?"
Jesus asked this one day as he came on the scene and heard the story.
And, on the surface, the question sound absurd.
Who wouldn't want to be healed?
Do you ask a starving person if he wants a meal?

124

or a pauper if he needs any money?

But then, why does the question seem important?
   Why is it a question to me and not only to a
   paralytic?
      Why does it haunt me so?
Is it possible that I and many of my comrades are sick,
   not because the circumstances are always stacked
   against us out around the pool,
      but because deep down inside we really don't want to
      be healed?

Maybe there are benefits in *not* getting to the pool first,
   and that Jesus knows this,
      and wants us to know it too.
In that case, the question leaps off the page,
   and out of the past,
   and demands an answer.

For instance, continued sickness is not a bad way to
punish ourselves.
We carry a great deal of guilt.
We have feelings of inferiority.
   We didn't do right,
      We didn't have what it takes,
         We really deserve to be beaten.
So . . . we might live with paralysis as *quid pro quo.*
Be sick for thirty-eight years . . . and be saved!

This is man-made atonement.
It is not in touch with the old song "Jesus Paid It All."
It is quite the reverse.
It's almost as if we were saying, though unconsciously,
   "Give me my paralysis, and I'll pay my own way."
No wonder Jesus says, "Do you want to be healed?"

Or, look at the question another way.
Yonder at the Sheep Gate, and beyond the pool of
Bethzatha, is the market.

It teems with people coping as best they can with life.
They drive caravans,
　jostle with camels,
　　haggle with tax collectors,
　　　make some shekels,
　　　　gain some prominence,
　struggle with sweat-of-the-brow existence.
Who expects this of a paralytic?
Nobody expects success of him . . . or failure.
Climb the ladder of success? How? With paralyzed feet?

Not bad!
Out from under, and with a good excuse,
　　　　and with sympathy as a recompense.

Again Jesus presses the question, "Do you want to be
healed?"
　"Really healed?"
　　"Even when it means being jostled in the
　　marketplace?"

Or, a further possibility:
A thirty-eight-year illness can be a clever way to
manipulate.
Some, by mournful voice and soulful gaze, turn
weakness into a claim.
They exert unusual power over the healthy,
　turn weakness to sick advantage,
　　prey on sympathies,
　　　gain attention,
　　　　demonstrate what someone called "the tyranny
　　　　of goodness."

Amazing, the uses of paralysis.
Enough that to escape from paralysis is not a
self-evident desire.
Hence the question. The probing question,
　aimed to penetrate our defenses,
　　waiting for a deeper answer.

Do you want to be healed?

Suppose you say yes—and really mean it?
What can Jesus do for you?
What would the miracle be?

This can't really be answered in advance.
Every cure is specific,
    as specific as the illness.
For some, it may be a physical act of healing
    as real and complete as that of the paralytic's,
    a cure that permits you to take up your bed and
    walk.
After all, a high percentage of physical illness has a
psychological base.
A lot of illness might be within reach of a
not-too-extraordinary faith.
Perhaps it is only a mind-set that prevents you from
going the short distance to the pool.

Elizabeth Barrett was an invalid when the family lived
on Wimpole Street,
    shut up in a room by an overprotective father.
Then, she felt the love and exuberance of Robert
Browning.
    His faith in her
        and love for her made the difference.
Months after their elopement, she was climbing hills in
Italy.
The paralysis was gone.

But, physical healing is not for everyone.
Not all illness, weakness, imperfection will go away,
                                    or needs to.

The greater miracle may not be the physical healing.
It may instead be the ability to leave the portico,
    to get back into life,

to accept the paralysis and still get away from the
pool.

Consider—How many Biblical people did *not* get
healed, and yet were healthy and useful?

Jacob limped, and grasped God's blessing.
Moses stuttered, and led an exodus.
Hosea got divorced, and found his vocation,
Paul had a thorn in the flesh, and learned more about
grace.

All of them apparently wanted to be healed,
at least enough to get off their beds,
and leave the portico,
and get back into life.

Thornton Wilder develops this theme in his play, *The
Angel Who Troubled the Waters.*
The paralytic complains, "If only I did not have this
illness, I'd show you what I could do for God."
To which the angel responds, "Without your wound,
where would your power be?"
No one can move the hearts of other people
more than someone
who has been broken on the wheels of living.

So, the question of Jesus is not nonsense.
That's why it stands in our path,
and points a finger at each of us,
and demands an answer.

We all have our weaknesses, and paralysis.
Some have had these for thirty-eight years and more.
But listen—Do you want to be healed?
Enough so that you can leave your pallet?

"The fault, dear Brutus, is not in our stars,
but in ourselves, that we are underlings."

THE ABSURD GOODNESS OF GOD

Matthew 20:1–16

The story of the laborers in the vineyard has enough
absurdities built in that it could be a slice of life seen by
those who feel life is ultimately unfair.

Or, is it the reverse?

Is it another slice of life?
  The slice seen by those who know they've gotten far
  more than they deserve?

Which is it, this story?
Is the God pictured here absurdly good?
      or just absurd?

Certainly there's absurdity in the story.
The more it's made to teach about economics or labor
practice,
    the more absurd it appears.
Any business person who tried to put this teaching into
practice
    wouldn't last a year.

It's late summer,
  rains are coming,
    grapes need harvesting.
The workday begins at 6 A.M.

The owner goes to the labor hall, says to a group,

129

"Looking for work?" and they answer yes.
  "Fine!"
      "There's the vineyard. Go pick grapes."
          "And, let's agree to one denarius a day."
(A denarius, by the way, was the average pay for a
day's work.)

They go and work.

The owner goes out again, and again,
    at nine o'clock, noon, three o'clock, five.
At these times, no contract is made.
The men are there who need work, and want work.
The owner simply says, "Go out, work,
and rest assured,
    I'll do what is right by you."

Six o'clock, the whistle blows.
The owner comes and, following Jewish custom, pays
each man for the day.
    The late afternoon group—a full day's pay, one
    denarius.
    The three-hour workers—a full day's pay, one
    denarius
    The six-hour group—the same.
Finally, the last group came—those under contract.

They had worked twelve hard hours,
    sunup to sundown,
        doing strenuous, backbreaking work.
And what did they receive?
                        One denarius—a full day's pay.

Naturally, they were ticked off.
What's this? Our work valued the same as the
Johnny-come-latelies?"
    "Unfair!" "Unfair!"
        "Where's George Meany? Cesar Chavez?"
            "Start the boycott! Throw up the picket lines!"

Then, the landlord speaks.

"Have I really been unfair?"
    "Didn't we have a contract?"
        "Didn't I keep my bargain?"

"And, furthermore, can't I be generous?"
"If I'm quite fair to you, can't I be quite generous to
others?"

"Well, yes . . ." (There is some mumbling as the
workers sort this out.)
"Yes," they concede, "we suppose so,
    But frankly, what a way to run a railroad!"

That's the story as Jesus told it.
It's certainly a strange one.
If this is a lesson in labor relations, my sympathies are
with the all-day workers.
If this landlord were operating in the San Joaquin
Valley,
    A boycott and a good strong union would be called
    for.

There's too much unfairness in the work world now.

For consider:
I work hard,
    do my best,
        give an honest day's work for a day's pay.

And, from my observation, there are a lot of inequities.
    Mazie is always taking sick days off whether she
    needs them or not;
    Muriel goofs off at the water fountain or coffee
    machine;
    Mac is the world's best delegator:
        He simply passes the work on.
Come payday—they all get the same as I do, if not
more.

And, have you noticed those right out of college?
Their salary starts where mine ended after years of
experience.
These Johnny-come-lately whiz kids!
Life should be fair.
But it isn't.

I'd like to believe that if you do right from 6 A.M. until
6 P.M.
you'll make out better than those late afternoon types
that put in an hour just before the whistle blows.
But it doesn't happen.

Don Wilson, a brilliant, compassionate pastor,
head of a large church in Lancaster, Pennsylvania,
forced to resign. Hit with cancer.

A certain woman, now divorced:
She tried to do right.
Did she deserve to be left with the kids,
while he took up with another woman?

A middle-aged child living near senile parents,
directly responsible for their well-being.
The other children are states away, in Southern
California.
How convenient for them!

And consider those rascals who never have trouble.
They have no great faith,
no great goodness.
Why is their paycheck the same as mine? Unfair!

If you are identifying with the 6 A.M. workers, as I tend
to do,
that is your slice of life.
Life has inequities,
Life is unfair!

But, suppose the story is not about economics at all.

Suppose we are not the 6 A.M. workers, but more like
those called in for the last hour?
Suppose we are not dealing with a landlord of strict
justice,
    but one of absurd generosity?
Just suppose we're in the hands of a taskmaster who,
    admittedly in a crazy way,
        gives far more than any deserve,
            and that we are among the undeserving,
                and not among those who are "earning" their
                way?
Then, the story is completely different.
Then God—for that is who the landlord represents—is
of a nature to be more good than fair.

And this is what the story seems to teach.

While the 6 A.M. workers use their calculators to see if
they got all that's coming,
We who have more savvy to the ways of God,
    and who should know the real score,
        should go home with a full day's pay,
            humming "Amazing Grace."

Honestly now,
If we really size up how we've fared,
    haven't we gotten more than we deserve?
        Absurdly so?

Two retired men came to joyful and useful faith in my
last church.
One was president of the Trustees; the other an Elder.
The Elder was also a "man Friday" in the office.
Both came to faith past fifty-five, and had a great time
in the church.

    Was their experience a recompense for fifty-five years
    of devotion?
    Or was it the touch of the landowner?

The absurd goodness of God?

Eric Hoffer, early in his working life, picked up a used
copy of Montaigne's essays,
    became fascinated by a well-constructed sentence,
        was led on to a goal: Be a writer.

Did this happen by chance? by serendipity?
Or was it another mark of an absurdly good landlord?

And what more could be said:
    about the time Murphy's Law did not operate,
        when grace worked in our homes, despite the fact
      we didn't follow Spock or Gesell,
           and when we didn't reap the consequences of our
           misadventures.

As a psalmist phrased it, "If thou, O LORD, shouldst
mark iniquities, LORD, who could stand?
But there is forgiveness with thee . . ."

    absurd mercy,

    that follows us all the days of our life:

    Late afternoon people who get paid absurdly well.

So, let the calculating types continue to work under
contract,
    and find ways that life is unfair.
They can make their case quite well.
But frankly,
    "High heaven hates the lore
    Of nicely calculated less or more."

God's essence is not strict fairness.

The heart of the eternal is most wonderfully kind.

There is a crazy generosity there,
And of this bounty we have all received.

KEEP UP THE GOOD WORK

Hebrews 12:1–2

Perhaps we'd better begin by putting Hebrews 12 against its background.

By faith: Abel offered a more acceptable sacrifice
Noah took heed and constructed an ark
Abraham obeyed and went out, not knowing where
Isaac invoked future blessings on Jacob and Esau
Joseph made mention of the exodus
Moses refused to be called the son of Pharaoh's daughter . . .

"And what more shall I say? For time would fail me to tell of Gideon, Barak, Samson, Jephthah, of David and Samuel and the prophets—who through faith conquered kingdoms, enforced justice, received promises, stopped the mouths of lions, quenched raging fire, escaped the edge of the sword, won strength out of weakness . . ."

"Therefore, since we are surrounded by so great a cloud of witnesses, let us also lay aside every weight, and sin which clings so closely, and let us run with perseverance the race that is set before us, looking to Jesus . . ."

135

Believe it or not, all this Scripture is directed to a very
modern problem.
The congregation back then was not showing up for
worship,
   not displaying persistence in discipleship.
So, the writer drew a picture to prod them along.

The picture is of an amphitheater.
The contestants are on the field, and they are Christians
like you and me.
The "race" is the struggle to be faithful to Christ,
        to work for justice,
          show compassion,
            bring healing,
              speak a word of witness.
And the stands are cheering this kind of persistence.

The stands are filled with spectators. Witnesses.
   Abraham is there, and so is Isaac and Jacob.
     In section "E" are Isaiah and Jeremiah,
       On the other side are Rahab and Samson.
And they are all looking at what is going on out on the
field!
And they are cheering. "Go-o-o-o Church!"

The competitors are not looking at the stands.
Runners who look into the stands might run into a
wall.
They hear the cheers,
   and need them,
     but their eye is on the goal.
They are "looking unto Jesus the pioneer and perfecter
of our faith."

The reason the writer drew the picture is plainly stated.
He—or she—felt that persistence comes when we keep
in touch with those who ran the race before us,
   Who are still spectators of the new generation.

And that's right, for this is how it works.

Recently, my wife and I attended a performance at
Philadelphia's Academy of Music.
A pianist, John Browning, strode on stage, sat at the
Steinway,
   and immediately conveyed the excitement of Samuel
   Barber's *Concerto for Piano and Orchestra.*

At the conclusion, the audience erupted into applause.
Browning embraced conductor Eugene Ormandy,
Both waved kudos to the orchestra, then bowed.
Then, both looked and applauded the man in the box at
stage right.

In a few moments, Samuel Barber left the box, and
walked on stage.

Now, Browning doesn't need Barber's presence to play
well.
He and Ormandy caught the spirit of the music;
   conveyed it to the audience at the Academy.
But, what an added incentive to play their best!
Barber was looking on,
   with the sympathy a composer has for his
   composition,
      and the encouragement he has for those who
      perform it.
The fire of the performance was nurtured in the
presence of the "witness."

Whoever wrote Hebrews wanted Christians to know
   and feel the power of
      the witnesses.
There in the stands, and all around, were Abraham,
Isaac, Jacob,
         Gideon and Samson,
            Rahab and Ruth.

Therefore, since we are surrounded by so great a
cloud of witnesses, let us lay aside every weight, and
sin which clings so closely, and let us run with
perseverance the race that is set before us, looking to
Jesus . . .

Persistence is an unsung virtue of the Christian faith.
On the other hand, falling away,
                          giving up,
                              dropping out,
    describe a sin we do not always identify as a sin.

Keep on with it!
That's what the stands want to see demonstrated.
    That's what makes them cheer.

Now, for a moment, look around.
What kind of people are in the stands?
    What kind of race did they run?
There are facts about the throng that encourage
persistence.
For instance, not one of them was perfect.
They wasted no energy bemoaning that fact,
    nor did they think they were disqualified simply
    because of their flaws.
They appear, warts and all, and proceed to act
faithfully.

        Rahab was nicknamed "the harlot,"
        David was lusty in his own way.
        And Samson? He didn't visit Delilah just to play
            Scrabble.

        Abraham lied to save his skin,
        Jacob's name means "Deceiver,"
        And Joseph as a child was a spoiled brat.

Yet, they conquered kingdoms, enforced justice, received
promises.

They managed to find forgiveness, and ways of being
faithful.
They kept going lap after lap.

Or, consider this aspect of the crowd in the bleachers.
Very few of them got what we would call a "square
deal."
Yet, they didn't use that fact to start dropping out.

On the basis of another type of philosophy, they might
have.
Suppose they had reasoned that if they were "with it"
for God
    they'd be lucky in love,
        successful in business,
            better in health,
                free of misfortune . . .
What might they have done when the walls caved in?

What do you do when you don't get the breaks?
    Believe harder?
        Blame God?
            Forget religion?
These are some of the possibilities if you buy the
philosophy that
    the faithful are the lucky.

The bleachers crowd of Hebrews 11 was faithful, but
horribly unlucky by any human standard:

"Some were tortured. . . . Others suffered mocking
and scourging, and even chains and imprisonment.
They were stoned, they were sawn in two, they were
killed with the sword; they went about in skins of
sheep and goats, destitute, afflicted, ill-treated—of
whom the world was not worthy . . ."

And yet, this group kept in the race because they never
bought the philosophy that they should be lucky.

"Therefore, since we are surrounded by so great
a cloud of witnesses . . . let us run with perseverance . . ."

And this final observation about the crowd in the
stands.
They never completed the work they dreamed of,
   and yet they kept at their work.

They greeted the promises from afar,
   kept seeking a homeland,
      kept looking for the city with foundations.
         But
These all died in faith, not having received what was
promised.
That takes real stamina.

The hardest job is to deal with unending tasks.
Short assignments can be taken in stride.

If you felt the assignment might be completed the day
after next,
   you might find energy for that.

If in one year you could fight the "war to end war,"
   you could scrape and save and pay the price.
Short-term possibilities bring out this kind of heroism.

But, really now, how many battles are of this sort?

Most personal problems, to say nothing of world
problems, are pesky.
They don't go away in one or two battles,
They require a lifetime of plugging away.

There are victories, to be sure,
   but they are partial
      and often mixed with compromise.

What, then, shall we do?

Cop out?
Grow cynical?
They didn't—those people in the stands.

Therefore, since we are surrounded by so great a
cloud of witnesses . . . let us run with perseverance
the race that is set before us . . ."

Recently, I officiated at a wedding in another church.
One of our young men married a woman of the other
church.
During the reception, I learned the bride had a twin
sister.
Her father told me that four years ago, when the twin
was home for the holidays, she collapsed.

They rushed her to the hospital,
    did all they could,
        worked on her all night, to no avail.
She had a brain aneurism and she died.

Her father described the shock   and the grief,
    and the efforts to put life back together again.
He talked of the Christian community around them;
their support;
    the influence of their pastor, who stayed the night
    with them.
And little by little, he told of the family's reentry into
life.

Throughout the reception, several took me aside to tell
the same story,
    as if I were a stranger to the tale.
Then these others added,
    "The way the family handled it was an
    encouragement to us all."

That's running with perseverance the race set before us.

There are countless other ways of running,
    lap after lap,
        day after day.

And whenever that dogged persistence is on display on
the field,
    the cheering begins in the stands.
It begins in the royal box and sweeps through the
bleachers,
    and on up, up,
        and into the clouds.

"Therefore, since we are surrounded by so great a
cloud of witnesses, let us also lay aside every weight,
and sin which clings so closely, and let us run with
perseverance the race that is set before us, looking to
Jesus the pioneer and perfecter of our faith, who for
the joy that was set before him endured the cross,
despising the shame, and is seated at the right hand
of the throne of God."

NOTES

1. Virginia Brasier, "Time of the Mad Atom," reprinted from *The Saturday Evening Post,* May 28, 1949, p. 72; © 1949 The Curtis Publishing Company.

2. Joseph Sittler, "Space and Time in the American Religious Experience," *Interpretation,* Vol. XXX, No. 1 (Jan. 1976), pp. 44–52.

3. Ibid., p. 48.

4. Ibid., p. 47.

5. *The Unchurched American:* A Study Conducted by The Princeton Religion Research Center and The Gallup Organization, Inc. (Princeton, N.J., 1978), pp. 15, 17.

6. T. S. Eliot, "Choruses from *The Rock,*" I; *The Complete Poems and Plays 1909–1950* (Harcourt Brace & Co., 1952), p. 96.

7. Anthony Trollope, *Barchester Towers* (1857; Doubleday & Co., 1945), pp. 49–50.

8. Johannes C. Hoekendijk, *The Church Inside Out* (Westminster Press, 1966), p. 65.

9. Marianne Moore, *Predilections* (Viking Press, 1955), p. 3.

10. Ibid.

11. Dorothy Sayers, *The Poetry of Search and the Poetry of Statement* (London: Victor Gollancz, 1963), p. 281.

12. T. S. Eliot, *Four Quartets,* "Burnt Norton," V; *The Complete Poems and Plays 1909–1950,* p. 121.

13. T. S. Eliot, *Four Quartets,* "East Coker," V; *The Complete Poems and Plays 1909–1950,* p. 128. See also Sayers, *The Poetry of Search and the Poetry of Statement,* p. 270.

14. James Baldwin, *The Fire Next Time* (Dial Press, 1963).

15. Adapted from Carl Sandburg, *Abraham Lincoln: The War Years,* Vol. II (Charles Scribner's Sons, 1939), pp. 452–477.

16. Donald A. Stauffer, *The Nature of Poetry* (W. W. Norton & Co.,

1946), pp. 22–25. The stanzas quoted are from A. E. Housman, *A Shropshire Lad*, XL.

17. Jonathan Price, "Words," in *Harper's*, Vol. 248 (March 1974), p. 10.

18. Friedrich Nietzsche, commenting on his "Thus Spoke Zarathustra" in *Ecce Homo;* quoted in D. Bruce Lockerbie, *The Liberating Word* (Wm. B. Eerdmans Publishing Co., 1974), p. 34.

19. James T. Cleland, *Preaching to Be Understood* (Abingdon Press, 1965), p. 100.

20. Stauffer, *The Nature of Poetry*, p. 61.

21. G. Ernest Wright, *God Who Acts* (London: SCM Press, 1952), p. 107.

22. Edmund A. Steimle, *From Death to Birth* (Fortress Press, 1973), p. 65. The quotation is from *W. H. Auden: Collected Poems*, edited by Edward Mendelson (Random House, 1976), p. 140. Copyright 1940 by W. H. Auden. Reprinted by permission of Random House, Inc.

23. Henry Grady Davis, *Design for Preaching* (Muhlenberg Press, 1958), p. 268. All pronouns have been changed to the plural.

24. Ibid., p. 269.

25. This illustration is used in Peter Farb's *Word Play* (Alfred A. Knopf, 1974), p. 139.

26. Davis, *Design for Preaching*, p. 269.

27. Steimle, *From Death to Birth*, p. 73.

28. T. S. Eliot, *The Waste Land*, III, "The Fire Sermon"; *The Complete Poems and Plays 1909–1950*, p. 44.

29. Sandburg, *Abraham Lincoln: The War Years*, Vol. II, p. 472.

30. Robert Evans, quoted in *Context* (Martin E. Marty, ed.), June 1, 1978, p. 3.

31. Ibid.

32. Catherine Drinker Bowen, *The Most Dangerous Man in America* (Little, Brown & Co., 1974), p. 90.

33. Catherine Drinker Bowen, *The Writing of Biography* (The Writer, 1950), p. 28.

34. Martin E. Marty, *Righteous Empire* (Dial Press, 1970); see also Dean R. Hoge, *Division in the Protestant House* (Westminster Press, 1976), pp. 74ff.

35. Paul Sherry (ed.), *The Riverside Preachers* (Pilgrim Press, 1979).

36. Rod MacLeish, *The Guilty Bystander* (Fortress Press, 1971).

37. B. Davie Napier, *Come Sweet Death* (United Church Press, 1967).